An overview of the grid during the start of the 84th running of the Le Mans 24 Hours on June 18, 2016.
GERLACH DELISSEN/CORBIS VIA GETTY IMAGES

WELCOME TO
100 YEARS OF LE MANS

There is simply nothing quite like it anywhere in the world. The Le Mans 24 Hours is unique in so many ways. Sure, there are other 24-hour endurance races on the international calendar and other races that are older. But none have the mixture of appeal that makes Le Mans so special.

It's a race of incredible speed, endurance, engineering and danger, a place where only the most unflinchingly brave succeed. Legends have been made and lost on the streets of La Sarthe over the course of the last century.

The event's mixture of using permanent race circuit with public roads, with cars repeatedly topping 200mph every lap, makes it an incredible challenge for drivers, teams, engineers and manufacturers, as does La Sarthe's notoriously unpredictable climate. Anything can, and usually does, happen at Le Mans. One second you can be in control, the next... *bang*... trouble can strike at any turn and there's a lot of them around the 8.5-mile Circuit de la Sarthe.

The sheer unpredictability keeps people coming back, along with hundreds of thousands of fans from across the world. Le Mans goes beyond just being another motor race, with concerts, fan villages and entire communities drawing together to create a festival atmosphere for an entire week in Central France. From public scrutineering in the shadow of the wonderful 14th century Saint Julian Le Mans Cathedral, where cars are cheered out of trucks like rock stars, to the driver parade through town, Le Mans does an incredible job of bringing racing to the people.

And when things get serious, there are few feelings like pressing your face to the fencing to catch the glow of brake discs in the dead of night as the cars relentlessly pound on, the aroma of hot rubber mixing with that of hundreds of barbecues.

From its early days of running as a simple production car trial on rough and pitted roads (which as you will read is also unique, considering it had no winner for the first three years!) to the modern times of space-age hypersonic prototypes,

Le Mans has witnessed an incredible rate of change. It's now a flat-out 24-hour sprint race, with zero room for error. It all adds to the addiction.

Yet, no matter how much Le Mans has changed and progressed, it still essentially holds the same appeal. Drivers and manufacturers continue to flock here because it is simply the biggest and the toughest race in the world to win. Even those who have conquered it will happily admit that if Lady Luck doesn't favour you at Le Mans, you've got no chance.

Within this special issue, we'll take a tour across the different stages of the race, uncovering the best stories from each era, together with the heroes, villains and machinery that helped make the legend.

And, as the Le Mans 24 Hours approaches its 91st Edition this summer, the rise of the new Hypercar era promises to bring back the glory days of sportscar racing. And we cannot wait to see it.

Enjoy.

Robert Ladbrook

MAIN COVER IMAGE: PORSCHE AG. HERE: THE TRADITIONAL LE MANS START IN 1965

CONTENTS

ISBN: 978 1 80282 742 2
Editor: Robert Ladbrook
Contributing editors: Jim Weeks, Eric Dymock
Imagery: Getty Images, Porsche AG, Audi Sport, Toyota Gazoo Racing, AC Heritage, Jaguar Heritage, Mazda, McLaren, Newspress
Senior editor, specials: Roger Mortimer
Email: roger.mortimer@keypublishing.com
Cover design: Dan Hilliard
Design: SJmagic DESIGN SERVICES, India
Advertising Sales Manager: Brodie Baxter
Email: brodie.baxter@keypublishing.com
Tel: 01780 755131
Advertising Production: Debi McGowan
Email: debi.mcgowan@keypublishing.com

SUBSCRIPTION/MAIL ORDER
Key Publishing Ltd, PO Box 300, Stamford, Lincs, PE9 1NA
Tel: 01780 480404
Subscriptions email: subs@keypublishing.com

Mail Order email: orders@keypublishing.com
Website: www.keypublishing.com/shop

PUBLISHING
Group CEO: Adrian Cox
Publisher, Books and Bookazines: Jonathan Jackson
Published by
Key Publishing Ltd, PO Box 100, Stamford, Lincs, PE9 1XQ
Tel: 01780 755131
Website: www.keypublishing.com

PRINTING
Precision Colour Printing Ltd, Haldane, Halesfield 1, Telford, Shropshire. TF7 4QQ

DISTRIBUTION
Seymour Distribution Ltd, 2 Poultry Avenue, London, EC1A 9PU
Enquiries Line: 02074 294000.

The Le Mans 24 Hours. Simple in theory, but perhaps motor racing's most challenging event. PORSCHE AG

THE ULTIMATE
CHALLENGE

The Le Mans 24 Hours is legendary for being an extreme test for the world's best drivers, teams, and cars. So, what does it take to be able to compete at the front of the world's toughest endurance race?

The concept of the Le Mans 24 Hours has barely changed across the last 100 years and sounds so simple in its essence: get into a car and drive as fast as you can for an entire day.

But in doing so, both man and machine face a challenge like no other, one that pushes the finest engineering minds in the world to breaking point and the human body to the physical and mental limit.

Racing at Le Mans has been likened to many different things. Nigel Mansell said ahead of his debut in the 2010 race: "Le Mans is the most dangerous race in the world, but also the most exhilarating… it's exciting, worrying, daunting…" and this coming from a grizzled veteran of both Formula 1 and IndyCar. But danger is just one facet of the challenge of the Le Mans 24 Hours. The sheer mental and physical exertion required to make it to the finish is a much-overlooked factor, and the one that plays the heaviest on the drivers' minds.

The Circuit de la Sarthe itself isn't the most extreme of layouts, but the combination of permanent circuit and everyday public carriageways make for a test that's truly unique. Throw in often changeable weather conditions, fluctuating grip levels, the transition from day to night, plus the almost limitless variables that racing at over 200mph brings and you begin to get an idea of the task drivers face. Often the track, and the car, will be totally different each time they jump into it. Nothing at Le Mans is a given.

And then there's the engineering aspect. Cars surpass that 200mph barrier five times every

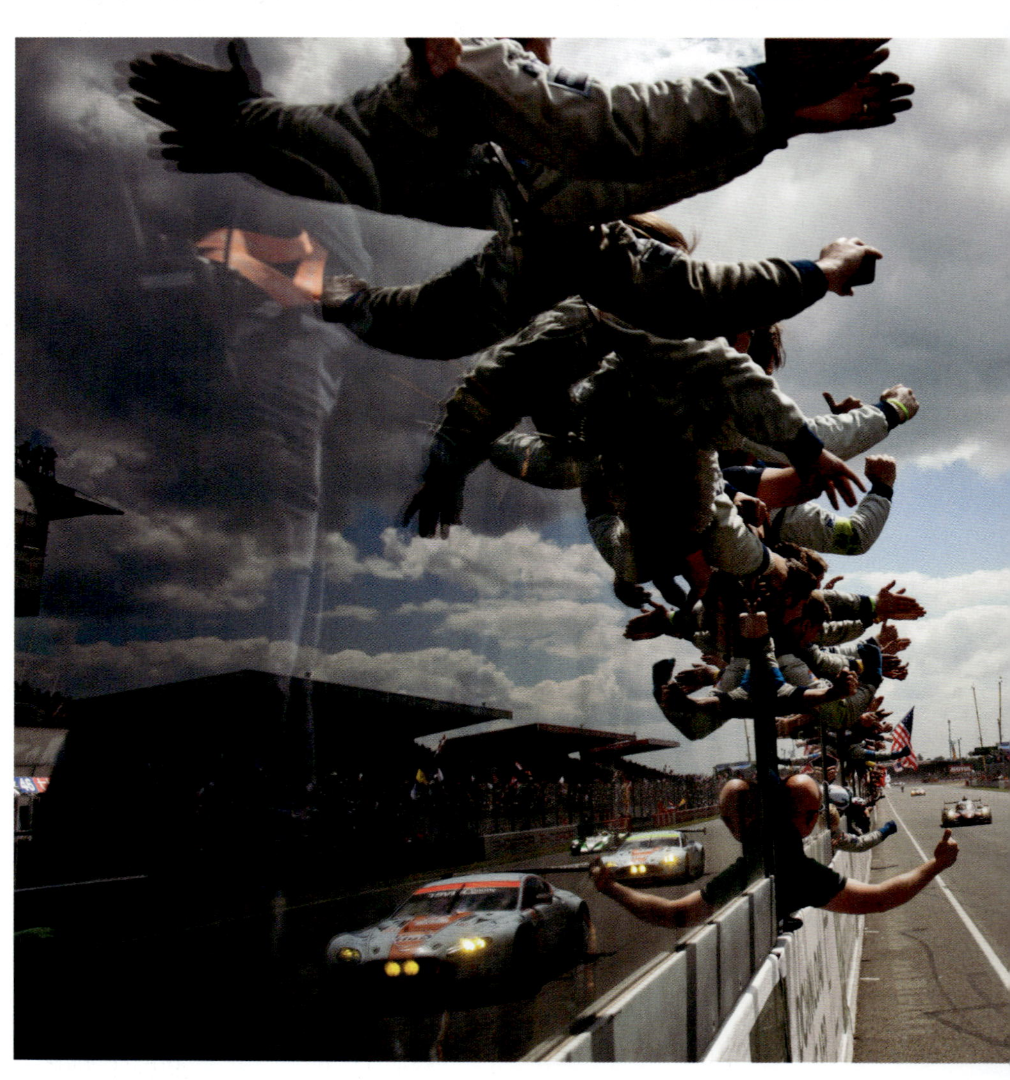

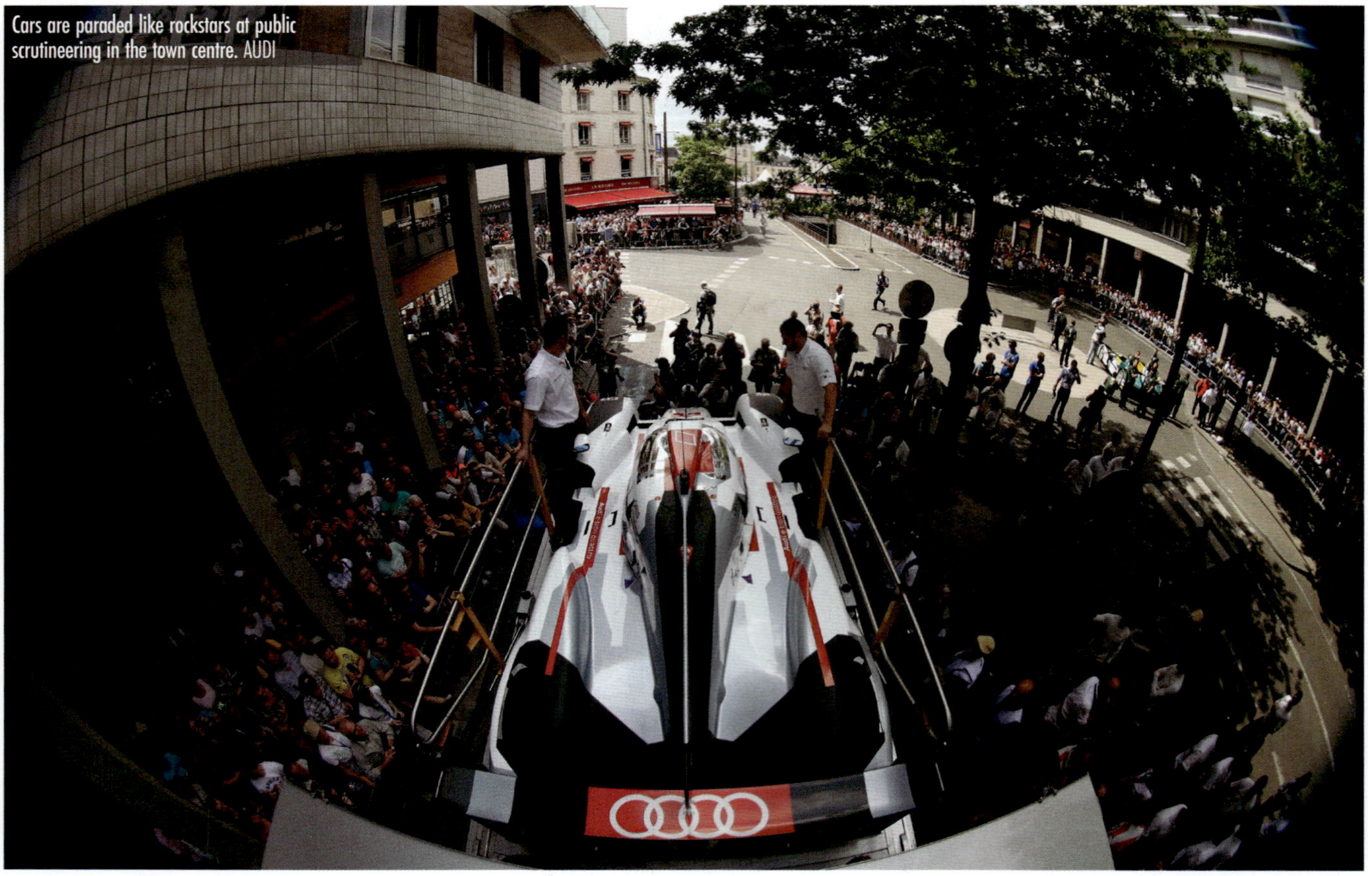

Cars are paraded like rockstars at public scrutineering in the town centre. AUDI

lap and there's typically around 380 laps across a modern race distance. When combined with the braking forces involved in slowing a racing prototype at the end of the fastest point of the track, the Mulsanne Straight, that's quite some punishment that both the car itself and the squidgy organic bit driving it has to withstand.

Tyres and suspension must be capable of coping with huge cornering forces over stints of up to four hours, while being battered with different grains and gradients of asphalt, plus the odd kerb bash as drivers inevitably push the limits to shave an extra tenth off a three-minute lap time.

Engines are required to complete more mileage than an entire Formula 1 season across a single day of racing at Le Mans, running non-stop in what has become a 24-hour sprint race during modern times as racing car technology has developed to cutting-edge point. Reliability must also be twinned with performance. But for many, simply finishing Le Mans can feel like a win, such are the multiple demands of the race.

"Le Mans is the toughest event for sportscar racing, it feels like the home of sportscar racing… the Mecca, and you can sense and feel the history of the place every time you arrive," said 'Mr Le Mans', Tom Kristensen, who has won the famous race a record nine times between 1997-2014.

"Any race at Le Mans is history, it's a place that gives huge adrenaline and demands extreme focus, and you have to try and stay as calm and alert as possible. A new chapter of history is always written at Le Mans each year."

The sheer scale of the event puts Le Mans head and shoulders above the rest of the motor racing calendar as the biggest race in the world, regularly drawing crowds of over 250,000 spectators to the Circuit de la Sarthe,

To even see the finish line takes incredible team effort. ASTON MARTIN RACING

TOP and ABOVE: Part of the challenge is the circuit's mixture of public roads and permanent race track. NEWSPRESS

while also commanding constant TV coverage around the world. That brings huge pressure on the entrants – both the drivers and teams – to perform in front of the watching world.

And that only heightens the danger aspect, with so many so keen to impress on the biggest stage of them all, anything can happen in an instant. Any race running for that long, on inconsistent roads, counts as a risk. And, with the speeds being so high at Le Mans, the fear factor becomes an issue for even the most experienced drivers.

Adapt, and adapt fast...

Formula 1 world champion Jenson Button is a case in point. Having completed over 300 grands prix, tackled the gruelling Baja 1000 off-road rally raid and flown high-powered rallycross cars off jumps, you'd think little would faze a man like Button. But his Le Mans debut in 2018 with the disappointing SMP Racing LMP1 prototype still came as a shock to the system. Button's car lost a lot of time with technical issues and eventually retired shortly before the finish, but it did give the 2009 world-beater a first taste of the 24 Hours.

"Le Mans was such as eye-opener for me, and actually I found it really stressful," Button said. "There's huge atmosphere, not just from the fans but also among the drivers, as you're all in the same situation, regardless of which class you're racing in. You're all there to do the same job and there's real camaraderie in that.

"The driving experience is very difficult. You spend such a long amount of time crunched up in a very small cockpit, but the adrenaline gets you through. But when you get out of the car your muscles tense up and it hurts like hell! I had several massages to try and stay loose through the race and I found it hard to wind down when I wasn't in the car. Sleeping was very tough, and if you're not getting adequate rest that adds a whole other dimension to the stress of it.

"And then there's the circuit. Our car was so pointy at the front end, so you'd drive down the Mulsanne – which is a normal A-road, let's not forget, with a centre point that drops away to the edge for drainage – and when you hit the centre point, the car would pull heavily to one side and you just had to guess which way it was going to go. But driving 350kph (217mph) at night was just amazing. Seeing that sun come up from the cockpit of a race car at Le Mans is something so special. I loved it."

Button experienced the full range of challenges as an endurance racing 'rookie', albeit a highly experienced rookie. However, his case shows how much drivers have to adapt to the specific requirements of Le Mans. Even the best have to learn. And learn fast.

Allan McNish was a star in single-seaters before beginning an ultra-successful endurance racing career with first Porsche and then Audi. He competed at La Sarthe 14 times, winning outright on three occasions. He remembers his first experience of the 24 Hours fondly.

"The driving style has to change in mentality," McNish said. "I was a selfish little person early in my career, largely because you had to be when racing formula cars. But it took a mentality change for me to grab hold of the fact that I now had a team-mate and it was actually beneficial if they were as quick, if not quicker, than me.

"Stephane Ortelli was my first team-mate and he would put his arm around me and give me a detailed run through the track and I'd never done that with a team-mate... ever! Teamwork was a lesson and it's key even today. If you listen to the teams, you can tell who's working as a unit, and who isn't... it's so obvious.

cope with the mental tests of being active for 24 hours. That brings specific dietary and training requirements for the modern racer.

Oliver Jarvis has made 11 Le Mans starts since his debut in 2010, finishing on the outright podium three times with Audi before then taking a shock second overall and an LMP2 class victory with the Jackie Chan DC Racing team in 2017. He says preparation for Le Mans starts well before race week, but only experience can truly settle the nerves.

"You take the same approach into the 24 Hours as you do into a six-hour World Endurance Championship race, but the biggest difference is you know that during a 6hr race you'll drive the car a maximum of twice, whereas when you finish a stint at Le Mans you are acutely aware that you have to get yourself focused and recuperated for the next time you get in the car," he explained.

"You have to go away and eat, drink, and try to sleep. In a 6hr race you can get out of the car and chill out, just watch the screens in the garage. You can't do that at Le Mans because you have to be fresh and energised all the time. If you don't eat or drink enough, it has a knock-on effect over 24 hours, it doesn't over six. You have to be ready for a stint the minute the driver before you goes in to start theirs, purely because it could be that they do an hour and have a problem and it's better for the strategy to switch drivers at the next stop. It means you're always on tiptoes and on standby for such a long time. The only respite you get is as soon as you get out of the car. When there's two drivers queued up to take over, you need to try and get some rest.

"One of the hardest parts is being able to switch off. It's something that comes with years of experience and even then, some drivers still really struggle. The best way to explain it is if you run 10km as fast as you can, then try to go straight to bed, your body won't have it because you're pumped and your pulse is up and your mind is focused. Then even when you're not in the car you still have a vested interest in it, you still care as it's your car, and the thought of not being in control of it can be tough." ⟳

LEFT and BELOW: Sunrise signals the end of the gruelling night stints but brings its own challenges with tiredness and often glare. AUDI

"It's difficult to describe how violent racing at Le Mans is. You get about 3.5*g* put through you in the first corner alone. It's not the most physical circuit, but in terms of the ferocity of the actions, it's really hard going. You need to be a well-oiled and efficient team and that all just comes from practice. Because Le Mans always throws up something unexpected. The car and the track changes so much during the course of the race, it's a living changing organism, from weather, to grip levels, to tyres and fuel loads, and you have to adapt to all of it."

The mental stress...

Together with the physical demands and the necessity for strong teamwork, drivers must also

Porsche makes an early morning pit stop, and the crew must be alert. PORSCHE AG

Fatigue can catch up with even the best drivers and teams. PORSCHE AG

There's also the sheer stress of representing a brand that is ploughing huge sums of money into a programme, both to prove it is better than the competition, but also often for marketing benefit. And there's no kudos that weighs heavier than a win at Le Mans.

Oliver Gavin was the beating heart of Corvette Racing's GT programme for almost two decades, with 18 of his 19 consecutive Le Mans starts made with the American manufacturer. Corvette traditionally hasn't been one for European racing, aside from Le Mans, which prompts its one trip across the Atlantic each season as the General Motors marque comes to take on its European rivals. Bedecked in yellow, Corvette has quite the Le Mans following with flags and merchandise stalls decking fans out in true American style. Gavin has celebrated five GT victories with the brand but understands the pressure.

"Everything has to be perfect at Le Mans, from the tyre strategy and performance, to the pit stops and the drivers' stints," said Gavin. "One puncture can ruin your race. Winning Le Mans also carries so much weight for the manufacturer, it's the highlight of the year and there's always so much riding on it. A victory there is used in marketing campaigns all year, and sometimes for years to come, so there's huge pressure to live up to as a driver. Fortunately, the team I've always had around me has been so supportive that you can block a lot of that out. But there are still times when you see the scale of the race and just think 'wow.'"

Le Mans can bring other, much more unwelcome, challenges. And Kristensen adds that there are some situations for which you simply cannot prepare. He was part of the winning crew in the 2013 race, the year that his Danish compatriot Allan Simonsen lost his life in a tragic accident when his Aston Martin crashed at Tertre Rouge corner on just the third lap. Simonsen's was the first death at Le Mans under racing conditions since Jo Gartner in 1986.

"Some moments when you look back when we've lost someone, friends, there have been some very testing times, such as when we lost Allan," added Kristensen. "Losing anybody is a terrible part of life and the sport can be rocked by it, but you still have to continue. That was very hard to take."

Diversity, for good and bad...

Another feature of Le Mans is the diversity of the grid. With four classes all competing within their own race, things tend to get busy right from the start. With the fastest Hypercars mixing it with LMP2 prototypes and GT cars crewed by both professionals and amateurs, there's often limited margin for error. The gulf in skill between one of the finest GT drivers on the planet aboard a factory-entered machine and a wealthy enthusiast who has bought a seat is all part and parcel of the race's charm and shows the draw being a Le Mans driver has.

However, safety is always a priority and only recently the race organisers had to step in to remove a struggling amateur driver from the remainder of the weekend following a spate of accidents during the practice sessions. While Le Mans may be a huge lure to aspiring racers, it can also bite hard.

Jarvis added that being aware of your surroundings at all times is crucial for a safe and successful 24 Hours: "There are a lot of technical aspects of the track where if you don't get it right, it does cost you. The first sector is very technical and the Porsche Curves have to be inch-perfect to get a top time. They are all about bravery. I wouldn't say they are all about taking risks, but you do have to take that little bit extra into there. But it bites hard if you get it wrong.

"It's risk for reward. If you're in traffic you can gain three or four seconds just by diving inside a GT car at the right moment. That's huge in any race. But it's probably the most dangerous place to overtake. You have to be so alert at all times. One of the key things about it is not just the different levels of cars but the different levels of drivers – from complete amateurs to fully paid works drivers and ex/current F1 guys. The crazy thing is that by the end of the race you know which specific cars are aware of you and which ones need to be given a wider berth."

The lure of Le Mans often draws in entries who have shone in other areas of sport. For example, Sir Chris Hoy, having conquered the velodrome to become one of Britain's most successful Olympic athletes, set his sights on proving himself at the top level on four wheels with an LMP2 entry in 2016.

"Le Mans was just the ultimate test for me and my driving career," said Hoy, who had raced sports prototypes successfully at national level before taking on Le Mans. "It's so different to anything else you can race. I found the traffic management a big thing, because you have such a mixture of machinery and ability. It's about understanding basic principles and not being indecisive with lines and movements. When there's a top-class prototype behind you, you stick to your line until it's past you. Or if you're going for the corner, you commit and go for it and let them know what you are doing with direct movements, not muck about and look unaware of them – that's when accidents can happen. The grip and traction the fastest cars have is phenomenal, so they come up on you really fast, often with dazzling headlights in your mirrors at night.

"The mental side of the race is challenging, but there are definitely some tricks from cycling that helped me. The biggest thing is focusing on what you have control of and can have an impact on and not worry about the stuff that could go wrong that you have no influence over. It's crucial to do that in traffic, or when coming into a fast corner in the dark trying to find your reference point for braking or turn-in and then thinking 'oh god there's a wall over there, what if I get this wrong or a wheel falls off right now...'

LEFT: Anthony Davidson. HERE (FROM TOP): Oliver Jarvis, Allan McNish and Sir Chris Hoy

"You just have to simplify things and only worry about the stuff you control. You also have to stay strong during those moments of doubt that we all have, such as just before the race when you begin to think of all the things that could possibly go wrong. I used to have those exact same moments just before I got on the bike for big events and they are normal things to happen, but you don't dwell on them or engage with them. You put them away and know that you've dealt with them before."

The influence of Lady Luck

There is one final element of success at the Le Mans 24 Hours that can prove decisive – luck. There's a long, long list of drivers who probably should have won Le Mans: Stirling Moss, Brian Redman, stoney-faced Vic Elford, 'Brilliant' Bob Wollek, Mario Andretti, and Swiss star Jo Siffert to name a few.

But perhaps Anthony Davidson should be added to that list. The ex-grand prix racer made a total of 13 Le Mans starts between 2003 and 2021 and drove for some of the finest works teams, such as Peugeot Sport and Toyota. While he appeared on the overall podium twice, a win never went his way. But it so nearly did in 2016, before the heartbreaking events of the final five minutes, where the Toyota TS050 Hybrid he was sharing ground to a halt from a comfortable lead just as it was about to start its final lap. Davidson would never come closer but will still go down as one of the finest prototype drivers never to have won the great race.

"It was [fellow Peugeot Sport driver] Alexander Wurz who once said to me 'You don't win Le Mans, Le Mans chooses its victor' and I never believed him at the time, but I've learned the hard way that it's absolutely true," said Davidson. "The one thing you really need at Le Mans is luck on your side and I never really had that. But when you think of the near-infinite amount of variables across a race that long, you could put together perfect stints all race and then the clutch fails, or the electrics pack in, or a tiny insignificant bit of debris flies up and cuts a tyre. Lady Luck has to be on your side to avoid all those things. It's part of winning Le Mans. You can have the best plan and strategy in the world, but there always has to be an element of good fortune too."

Amen to that...

Leena Gade, here being hoisted aloft by her team, became the first female race engineer to win the race with Audi Sport. AUDI SPORT

What about the cars…?

Aside from the stresses and strains the drivers go through, the cars also take one hell of a beating over the course of a Le Mans week, so much so that the vast majority get entirely stripped to pieces and rebuilt on the 'down day' before the race.

Up until that point, they'll have been wheeled out of the trucks like rock stars to an adoring crowd as thousands of spectators flock to the public scrutineering in the town square – a hugely popular event pre-Covid, which is now making a comeback.

Then, with several hours of practice and qualifying across the traditional slots of Wednesday and Thursday, all building up to that final qualifying thrash on Thursday night when conditions are often at their very best, most entries start to show a little wear and tear.

Preparation is key at Le Mans, but so is reaction. From a team's point of view, you have to be ready for anything.

"So much can happen, Le Mans is not about just being fast, it's about reliability, procedures…

The podium brings an outpouring of emotion for the lucky crews able to take centre stage. AUDI

so much can happen and you have to be ready, because always something does happen," said Alex Hitzinger, who was technical director for Porsche's 919 Hybrid LMP1 programme. "You rarely have a quiet race at Le Mans."

Leena Gade, who became the first female race engineer to win Le Mans when she oversaw the operation of the 2011 Audi R18 TDI, added: "There is no one secret to winning Le Mans. It's a mixture of attention to detail, experience, immaculate preparation, handling and looking after your drivers well. Le Mans is a huge team effort. Every single mechanic, engineer and driver has to pull together. You have so much advanced technology that helps you to try and read the race, but you always have to react in smart ways to every situation and not let yourself be irritated by small details or minor setbacks. You just have to keep going."

As previously mentioned, one of the biggest Le Mans upsets came in 2017 when the Jackie Chan DC team's Oreca LMP2 came close to beating the Porsche factory LMP1 squad to the

The Circuit de la Sarthe's famous Ferris wheel illuminates the dark circuit. PORSCHE AG

outright win after several of the top-class crews hit technical trouble. The Jackie Chan DC team was operated by British engineering outfit Jota Sport and its boss Sam Hignett knows a thing or two about running cars at Le Mans.

"The secret at Le Mans is all about preparation and a good old dose of luck," said Hignett. "So many things can stop a car, and so many insignificant things these days, with all the technology that's involved. All you need is a single fuse to pop and it can be game over. Even in that 2017 race, we had a dragging clutch from the early hours, then we had a small shunt on the front and we had to change the rear

Tom Kristensen is the most successful Le Mans driver of all-time, with nine victories

bodywork when the lights failed and we still almost won overall!

"There's so much data coming off these cars now that you have a constant flow of information about how parts are performing. A mechanical problem tends to start and get worse and worse. It's up to you as a team to be able to manage it and the drivers to manage it and hopefully you can make that decline plateau. That's what wins Le Mans ultimately.

"Preparation is so key, as is knowing the state of what you're putting out on track at any given time. The cars are completely rebuilt on the Friday before the race and that gives you time to inspect and rebuild those sub-assemblies, maybe run them for a few hours around an airfield to make sure everything is working as it should. The more detail you can put in and the more time you have, you're eradicating more and more things that could go wrong.

"Obviously, you can't do anything about accidents or debris, you just have to react to those, but it's down to the team to make the car reliable and it's down to the drivers to manage that and not put the car under any additional stress. If you can do all of the above, then you stand a chance at Le Mans."

Like we said, Le Mans sounds simple… right? ●

And to the winners, the spoils. NEWSPRESS

The Chenard & Walcker of André Lagache and René Leonard on its way to a historic first Le Mans victory. Sort of... GETTY IMAGES

ORIGINS OF THE GREATEST RACE

Now a mecca for car makers showcasing the finest racing technology in the world, the Le Mans 24 Hours has come a long way from the era of pitted roads and haybales. This is the story of the race's formative years.

How can you have a race with no winner? The simple answer is that you can't – but nobody told the Automobile Club de l'Ouest. So, what began life as a simple car endurance trial has gradually morphed into the most famous 24-hour race in the world, the Le Mans 24 Hours.

In fact, Le Mans was famous well before the 24 Hours, as the central French town had already played host to the world's first grand prix in 1906. There was even an endurance element to that, considering it was run using a rather daunting, roughly triangular 65-mile road course and a typical lap took a full hour.

Also organised by the ACO – with backing from the Automobile club de France – that event coined the very term 'grand prix', due to the organisers stumping up an enormous 45,000-franc prize fund, roughly £200,000 in today's money. That made it quite the 'grand prize' and the term has stuck ever since.

With the ACO already blazing a trail with both the scale and prestige of its early racing events, another contest was devised, the Rudge-Whitworth Triennial Cup, which would pit manufacturers against each other in the ultimate duel of reliability. Sponsored by the British bicycle and tyre manufacturer of the same name, the idea was to draw in as many different marques as possible to compete in a total of three 24-hour trials, one per year, and whichever brand most surpassed its predetermined target mileage over the three events would claim victory. Clever really, considering the format essentially guaranteed participation for three years.

Key Moments

1923	Original circuit iteration measures 17.3km
1924	Rules brought in mandating cars do at least 20 laps with their hoods up
1925	Running start first used. It would become a defining Le Mans tradition
1926	Winning car averages 100kph for the first time. First grandstands built
1928	The Pontlieue section of track is bypassed by the new Dunlop curve
1930	First female entry with Margeurite Mareuse and Odette Siko
1932	Tertre Rouge section added to the track

Therefore, the very first Le Mans 24 Hours, then known as the Grand Prix d'Endurance, in 1923 technically never had an official winner – and neither did the second or third, thanks to the competition format. Notionally somebody had to finish first and that fell to the French Chenard-Walcker team, its Type U3 15CV Sport being driven for 128 laps by André Lagache and René Léonard, four tours more than its nearest rival.

However, under the rules of the Cup, it was the diminutive 1.1-litre Salmson that finished down in 12th that actually led the competition. The former air-pump manufacturer-turned-cycle-car brand's VAL-3 completed a full 98 laps, having only been expected to manage 52.

Perhaps the least surprising thing about that very first Le Mans was that it was dominated by French entries. Of the 35 cars that started, 32 were French, with the only exceptions being two Belgian Excelsiors and a sole Bentley entered by Canadian war veteran Captain John Duff, who had almost literally twisted the British ➲

The race in 1935 looked a lot different to what we now know with rough roads and primitive technology. GETTY IMAGES

Cars set off for the 1934 edition. This would be a third win in a row for Luigi Chinetti. GETTY IMAGES

manufacturer's arm to get to the event, even borrowing Bentley's test driver Frank Clement for the occasion.

Perhaps more surprising is that of the 32 cars to start, 30 of them finished, which is remarkable given the racing conditions.

Different life

Life at Le Mans back in those formative days was far from what we know now, even if geographically there are still some familiarities. The makeshift pits, formed by wooden counters with canvas coverings, were basically where the polished buildings of today's main pit straight stand, but the circuit itself was very different.

Consisting of a 10.7-mile loop, a lap would begin with a lengthy charge straight into the heart of Pontlieue town, where cars would race down the narrow residential streets towards a tight hairpin before then looping back towards Tertre Rouge and taking a more familiar route around Mulsanne, Indianapolis and Arnage.

In the first race, that first sector run to Pontlieue would have been as long as the famed Mulsanne Straight itself. It's little wonder that format was scrapped after 1928, saving locals from being confined to their houses for the entirety of race week. While much of the area was redeveloped, echoes of the famous Pontlieue Hairpin linger, that section being one of the more developed parts of an otherwise very basic track. Some Acetyline floodlights were borrowed from the army to light certain parts of the course, but aside from that the drivers were on their own.

Much of the racing surface was not tarred, with cars having to negotiate loose, rough and often pothole-ridden roads, especially on the more rural single-track lanes around Arnage. Engineers would treat the roads with a mixture of gravel, dirt and tar as a short-term solution, but the rugged nature of the surface undoubtedly played a part in the outcome of that first event, with the Bentley hampered when stones flicked up from the road broke each of its headlights and then one holed the fuel tank on the 3-Litre Sport.

The finish in 1930, as Woolf Barnato and Glen Kidston's number 4 Bentley crosses the line for victory. NEWSPRESS

Repairs cost the car several laps and left it joint fourth in the order, 16 laps behind the 'winning' Chenard-Walcker. It's impossible to say if the Bentley could have overcome the homegrown contingent and scored the first-ever Le Mans victory for British engineering, but the event would certainly have been closer – and the evidence for that lay in the years to come.

Bentley would claim its first win a year later in 1924 as Duff and Clement returned, the pair snatching victory after Lagache/Léonard's Chenard-Walcker caught fire on the Mulsanne. Bentley's triumph against an otherwise entirely French entry (41 starters in total) brought international acclaim to Le Mans. This was not just an event for French drivers in French cars. Winning it gave any manufacturer bragging rights against what was at the time the biggest car industry in the world.

The following year, 15 non-French entries arrived. Le Mans was becoming a truly multi-national race, the place where car makers from around the world could come to showcase not

Captain John Duff and Frank Clement's Bentley 3-litre rounds the Pontlieue Hairpin during the first Le Mans in 1923. BENTLEY

The Bentleys of Duff/Clement (9) and Bertie Kensington-Moir/Dudley Benjafield (10) in the pits in 1925

just their performance and innovation, but their reliability.

While Lorraine-Dietrich bagged two victories on the bounce, the decade belonged firmly to Bentley, which would go on to celebrate a further four wins as 'The Bentley Boys' came to be the class of the field into the 1930s.

Technology's advance also led to some startling numbers. The first event in 1923 was run at an average speed of 57.21mph, but by 1929 that had risen to 73.63mph. Fast-forwarding to 1939, the average stood at 83.61mph, showing just how swiftly things accelerated during those early races.

New inventions

Innovation was also rife, with aerodynamic 'slipstreamer' bodywork, front-wheel drive, air-cooled engines and four-wheel hydraulic brakes all making appearances on cars. German machinery began to appear from 1930, following Mercedes-Benz's first entry, which enjoyed a spell in the lead before the SSK retired in the night with a failed dynamo. Odette Siko and Marguerite Mareuse also became the first female drivers to enter, piloting their Bugatti T40 to a fine seventh place.

And then came the Italians… well, sort of. The slippery Alfa Romeo 8C-2300 LM shone after Bentley withdrew amidst crippling financial strife that would lead to it being absorbed by Rolls-Royce. Even then, the Alfa was a private entry from Britons and the noted Bentley Boys, Earl Howe and Henry 'Tim' Birkin. With a straight-eight engine designed by the legendary Vittorio Jano and its lightweight body, the 8C would become the machine to beat until the mid 1930s.

After this came a period of significant disruption. First, the 1936 race was abandoned due to civil unrest and national strikes in the midst of political turmoil. Racing would resume in 1937, with time for two Bugatti victories to sandwich a Delahaye success, but that final Bugatti win in 1939 was secured against an ominous backdrop. Just three months after Jean-Pierre Wimille and Pierre Veyron took the chequered flag, Adolf Hitler's forces crossed the Polish border to begin the deadliest and most destructive war in history. And, as the Nazi war machine rolled across Europe, racing at Le Mans would fall silent for the next decade. ●

The start of the 1928 race. Safe to say spectator numbers have increased a fair bit since then. GETTY IMAGES

THE BENTLEY BOYS

If there's one definitive group of drivers that changed the face of the Le Mans 24 Hours more than any other during those formative years, these aristocratic adventurers were it.

From left: Frank Clement, Sir Henry Birkin and Woolf Barnato. GETTY IMAGES

Given their respective heritage and privileged social positions, it's all too easy to dismiss the original members of the Bentley Boys as pumped-up playboys just out to flaunt their wealth and get some kicks in cars. But you'd be wrong.

In fact, this group of amateur drivers were devout supporters of the Le Mans 24 Hours from its very first moments and also helped to make the race the multi-national event it is today. Not only did they push the Bentley brand to the forefront of the international sporting spotlight with their efforts, but they also blazed a trail for other 'have-a-go' heroes.

And heroes they were, for here was a group of enthusiasts who perhaps didn't expect to live long enough to be able to go racing at all. Each was involved in some way with the Great War, fighting for their country and their lives. And for some, it seemed like the war never really ended such was their lust for adventure and conquest, even when the fighting stopped. It's little wonder they got a kick out of a glass or six of champagne after the fast cars were parked up.

But tales of their partying and indulgence pale in comparison with those of their sporting and philanthropic pursuits. Between the years 1923 and 1930, they brought Bentley five Le Mans 24 Hours victories and even saved the very company they unwittingly set out to promote. And their legacy lives on to this day. In 2019, a road near the Circuit de la Sarthe was renamed Rue des Bentley Boys and the grained photos of the oil-stained drivers have come to define the early days of Le Mans, some 100 years on. It's not the Delages, Bugattis and Chenard-Walckers that were pushed to the front of that early era – and that's thanks to the Bentley Boys. These are the stories of the most prominent members.

Captain John Duff

Active years: 1923-1925
Best finish: 1st 1924

Put simply, if it hadn't been for the efforts of Canadian John Duff, the Bentley Boys as we know them wouldn't have existed – and perhaps neither would Bentley. It was, in fact, Duff who persuaded W.O Bentley to give Le Mans a try. W.O notably wasn't in favour of one of his cars going to Le Mans, putting the brand at risk of being embarrassed by the French. But Duff thought differently.

Born in China to Canadian parents, Duff was educated in Hamilton, Ontario, before returning to Kuling (now Guling). However, once Britain declared war on Germany in 1914, Duff travelled across Russia and then sailed to the UK to join the Army. While serving, he was badly wounded in the Third Battle of Ypres in Passchendaele and transported back to England for medical attention, where he met and eventually married his nurse.

Once recovered from his injuries, Duff established a car dealership, Duff & Aldington, and took up competition driving as a form of advertising. His chosen model was Bentley and, keen to convince W.O to support his dealership, he soon began chasing records at Brooklands aboard its cars.

One of his more daring, and bizarre, achievements came in 1922 when he set out to raise the 24-hour speed record at Brooklands. Split into two 12-hour stints because the track had to close at night to allow locals some respite, Duff completed the entire thing solo in a Bentley 3-Litre, despite suffering crippling

Frank Clement, W.O. Bentley and the lanky John Duff in the Le Mans pits. W.O. was famously against his cars running, but Duff persuaded him. BENTLEY

back pain at the end of the first stint and having to be helped from his car and into a soothing bath. Yet at the end he set a new average speed record of 86.52mph over 2,082 miles.

But it was another feat of endurance that caught his eye. When Duff heard of the forthcoming Grand Prix d'Endurance, he went straight to Bentley to try and secure a car. W.O. reluctantly loaned him the 3-Litre Sport that would stand as the sole British entry that year, together with test driver Frank Clement. However, W.O. refused to have much more to do with it until a last-minute pang of guilt caused him to make the trip to France to support the motley crew, armed only with what few spares they could carry.

It didn't take W.O long to fall in love with the race, saying: "By midnight, I was certain that this was the greatest race I had ever seen." Duff and Clement eventually fell victim to a holed fuel tank in that event and finished fourth, but upon their return a year later, together with a much better equipped Bentley team, they won by a clear lap.

After giving up racing following an accident in America in 1926, Duff established a fencing school and dabbled in stunt double work for Hollywood actors of the time, such as Gary Cooper. He eventually returned to England and his story ended when he was thrown from his horse while riding in the Epping Forest, being fatally injured at the age of 62.

Sir Henry 'Tim' Birkin

Active years: 1928-1932
Best finish: 1st 1929 and 1931

When it came to ingenuity, no Bentley Boy was willing to go further than Tim Birkin, who was solely responsible for the creation of Bentley's most famous classic racer, the 'Blower' Bentley.

Born into a wealthy family in Nottingham, Birkin gained the nickname 'Tim' early in life, ➲

Kidston lights himself a cigarette mid-celebration after his and Barnato's 1930 victory. BENTLEY

A Bentley advert showing the 'Business-Like' Le Mans Bentleys, 1929. BENTLEY

MT 3464, 6½ litre chassis LB 2332.
YW 5758, 4½ litre chassis TX 3246, body 1502.
YH 3196, 4½ litre chassis ST 3001.
Three of the business-like 1929 Le Mans Bentleys.

Such has been the impact of the Bentley Boys, they even now have a 'rue' dedicated to them at the modern circuit. BENTLEY

taken from the popular children's comic of the time, Tiger Tim, and it stuck with him ever after.

Having served as a fighter pilot in the Royal Flying Corps during World War One, Birkin contracted malaria during a stay in Palestine and only took up motor racing in 1921, competing sporadically at Brooklands, his trademark blue and white spotted scarf billowing as he went.

With a love of speed and a hunger for the adrenaline it brought, Birkin took his driving career far more seriously later in the decade, purchasing a 4.5-Litre and joining the already established Bentley Boys factory team at Le Mans for 1928. A year later, he would be teamed with Woolf Barnato aboard the new Speed Six, a specially constructed racing variant boasting a 6.5-litre inline six engine capable of 200bhp. Birkin and Barnato would lead the most dominant display yet at Le Mans, with Bentleys filling the first four places, led by their Speed Six.

But an issue arose. As Bentley sought more and more speed, it simply created larger and larger cars. The Speed Six was already 11 feet long, leading Ettore Bugatti to famously label it 'the world's fastest lorry'. Instead, Birkin devised a plan to supercharge the smaller, lighter 4.5-litre model but, when W.O refused, claiming it would 'pervert the engine's design', Birkin simply did it himself. Having convinced wealthy racehorse owner Dorothy Paget to back the project, Birkin set up his own engineering works to prove the concept.

Working with engineer Clive Gallop and the Amherst Villiers supercharger company, the 242bhp 'Blower' Bentley was born. Yet, to be accepted at Le Mans, the car had to have a true production variant, so Birkin convinced Bentley to produce 50 official examples so he could take the car to Le Mans. While by far the most famed Bentley of the era, the Blower never shone in endurance racing due to its mechanical fragility, with then Bentley racing boss Nobby Clarke saying: "The Blower eats plugs like a donkey eats hay." But it did prove a star elsewhere, with Birkin scoring a famous second place in the 1930 French Grand Prix at Pau and setting a new lap record of 137.96mph at Brooklands in 1932.

After Bentley eventually shut up shop, Birkin would win Le Mans again in 1931, alongside Earl Howe in an Alfa Romeo 8C, earning a letter of congratulation from Mussolini. His final start would be in 1932 and then shortly after tragedy would strike. While reaching for a cigarette lighter during a pit stop at the Triploi Grand Prix, Birkin burnt his arm on the exhaust of his Maserati. Opinion is split between septic shock or the underlying malaria infection as the cause of the wound worsening, but Birkin would die from the injury just a month later.

Woolf Barnato

Active years: 1928-1930
Best result: 1st 1928, 1929 and 1930

In the words of W.O. Bentley: "The best driver we ever had and, I consider, the best British driver of his day. He was the only driver in my knowledge who never made a mistake." A glowing reference, but you wouldn't have thought it to look at him.

Barnato was made from a different mould – powerful, stocky and looking every inch more a boxer than a racing driver. And he was, proving himself handy at heavyweight level when at Cambridge before enlisting with the Army to serve in the war. As the son of a diamond magnate, cash was not something Barnato was short of, so when he took up a sport, he dedicated himself to it. Aside from racing, he was a powerboat champion, owned a stable of successful racehorses, was a keen golfer and even played cricket to a county level.

Undoubtedly his best record came at Le Mans though, where he achieved a hat-trick that has still to be equalled to this day. Scoring his first 24 Hours victory alongside Bernard Rubin in the 4.5-litre, 'Babe' Barnato would go on to win with Birkin and then Glen Kidston in Speed Sixes for 1929 and 1930 respectively before calling it a day. His 100 percent record is unique in the history of the race.

When Bentley began to struggle financially in the middle of the decade, he bought the company and continued to finance its sporting pursuits until the Wall Street Crash put paid to the growth of the business. Even Barnato's wealth fell short of saving the marque and it was eventually bought out by Rolls-Royce, but not before Barnato had cannily bought himself a chunky stake in Rolls-Royce too.

After his racing career, Barnato served as Wing Commander with the Royal Air Force during World War Two and devoted himself to his business interests. He eventually died from complications with cancer at the age of 52 in 1948.

Glen Kidston

Active years: 1929-1930
Best result: 1st 1930

Certainly not the most famous name on this list, but undoubtedly the greatest story. Kidston was the very epitome of the live-fast-die-young mindset, willing to throw himself head first at any challenge, be it on the track or in the air. And it led to a short but remarkable life.

Kidston simply thrived on danger and therefore never seemed to steer clear of it, having survived multiple torpedoes, being sunk at sea and a plane crash.

The grandson of a metal and machinery merchant with significant interests in banking, Kidston enjoyed tremendous wealth and lived in London's Grosvenor Square in an apartment adjacent to Barnato, Birkin and Tim Ruben in an area of the city still colloquially known as Bentley Corner.

Aged just 15, Kidston signed up with the Royal Navy at the start of the war in 1914 and survived being torpedoed twice aboard armoured cruisers, HMS *Aboukir* and *Hogue* that year. He later served aboard the HMS *Orion* dreadnought in the Battle of Jutland before taking over command of H-class submarines, only for his X1 craft to develop a faulty depth gauge and become stuck on the seabed, eventually resurfacing hours after the crew had been presumed lost.

A keen amateur racer on both two wheels and four, Kidston tackled the Monte Carlo Rally, Isle of Man TT and grand prix events before making his Le Mans debut in 1929, finishing second in a 4.5-Litre alongside Jack Dunfee. But that was far from the most dramatic moment of his

year. That November, he was the sole survivor of a Lufthansa Junkers G24 air crash, which went down near Caterham during a scheduled flight from Croydon to Amsterdam. Kidston adopted the brace position and survived the initial impact, eventually kicking his way clear of the wrecked fuselage, his clothes alight, before dousing himself on the wet grass and then going back twice to check for survivors. All five others on the flight, including the co-pilot who had ejected, were killed.

He returned to Le Mans for 1930 and won, sharing a Speed Six with Barnato, emerging ahead by six laps when both the Mercedes and Birkin's 'Blowers' blew up. Barnato famously labelled him" "The beau ideal of a sportsman… the word 'fear' had been expunged from his dictionary."

Kidston's achievement-hunting not yet done, he embarked upon a record-breaking flight from Wiltshire to South Africa in 1931, completing the journey in just over six days, averaging 131mph. But there would be no return trip, as Kidston's luck finally ran out during a reconnaissance flight around the Drakensberg Mountains when his borrowed de Havilland Puss Moth broke up and crashed during a dust storm. He was just 32. ●

A classic Bentley 3-Litre of 1925. Back then you'd have to do a few laps with the hood up too. BENTLEY

A LEGEND REBORN

The 1949 Le Mans 24 Hours was significant for many reasons, not least the race's return after a 10-year wartime hiatus. For a new constructor named Ferrari, this was to be the start of an enduring love affair. By Jim Weeks.

On Tuesday May 8, 1945, a new era was dawning across Europe. World War Two was at an end following unconditional surrender by the decimated German forces, bringing almost six years of bloody conflict to a close and providing hope that life might soon return to normal.

But the Armistice did not signal an immediate resumption of pre-war existence, instead beginning a slow process by which life gradually adjusted to a new kind of reality. For an example of this, we need only look to the Le Mans 24 Hours. Though peace was declared in May of 1945, it would be another four years before the great race resumed.

The final pre-war running had taken place in June 1939, just months before conflict erupted and barely a year shy of the German occupation of France. Indeed, it is sobering to see the official programme for the 1939 race, which featured the flag of Nazi Germany flying alongside those of Great Britain, the United States and France. Jean-Pierre Wimille and Pierre Veyron secured victory driving a Type 57SC Bugatti and for a time, it seemed that they might go down in history as the last winners of the Le Mans 24 Hours.

When it came, the war had hit the La Sarthe circuit especially hard. The site was requisitioned as an air base, first by the RAF and subsequently the Luftwaffe, making it a primary objective for bombing. The Mulsanne straight, which the Germans used as a runway, was an especially obvious target. Later in the war, the site housed prisoners and landmines were laid to prevent escape.

As such, it was not simply case of sweeping up the debris and going motor racing. Considerable work was required to get the site into a suitable condition. This required an equally considerable injection of capital, which explains why work did not begin until February 1949. Helpfully, local politician Christian Pineau, who was the national minister of public

A historic race start! The Le Mans 24 Hours roars back to life after a decade away, with the Eugène Chabaud/Charles Pozzi Delahaye (3) front and centre. GETTY IMAGES

works and tourism, signed off on a government grant that allowed for the construction of new buildings and grandstands.

What eventually went up met a very high standard, prompting one British reporter to declare that the grandstands 'make those at Silverstone look pathetic'. Parts of the track were resurfaced and there were even new facilities for the press who 'were handsomely looked after in their lofty and extensive stand, where they sat at school desks and received food boxes and wine tickets at generous intervals'.

But it wasn't all fresh paint and pressroom frivolities. Some areas remained off limits as they were yet to be cleared of mines. Though the race was back on, reminders of why it had been absent for so long remained. Nevertheless, Le Mans 1949 drew a healthy entry of 52 cars, the majority coming from France (33) and Britain (15), with two from Czechoslovakia and one a piece from Italy and Belgium. There were several firsts, including debuts for prototypes and for diesel engines, while the Simca 8 made history as the first Le Mans entrant to be fitted with a radio.

But the most significant first – in retrospect, at least – was the arrival of Ferrari machinery

The return of the Le Mans 24 Hours brought a wonderful sense of normality back to La Sarthe after a 10-year absence. GETTY IMAGES

at Le Mans. This was not a full-blooded factory effort, however. In fact, the driving force behind the entry was Luigi Chinetti, an engineer-turned-driver who played a significant role in pre- and post-war motor racing. Italian-born, he'd decamped to Paris amid the rise of fascism and won his first appearance at Le Mans in 1932. A second victory followed in 1934, both coming at the wheel of Alfa Romeo machinery. Following the outbreak of war Chinetti travelled to America and remained there for the duration, eventually taking U.S. citizenship.

New beginnings

In 1949, he returned home to find his possessions in Paris lost. From there, he headed to Modena for a meeting with his old acquaintance Enzo Ferrari, who had struck out on his own shortly before the war. Chinetti wanted to race one of Ferrari's new 166 models at Le Mans and tried to convince Enzo of the benefits his brand would reap from a successful assault. But 'Il Commendatore' would not sanction a factory entry, doubting that the car was ready to withstand a full 24 hours.

Undeterred, Chinetti turned to the English aristocrat and racing enthusiast Lord Selsdon. Peter Mitchell-Thomson to his friends, he and Chinetti had won the Paris 12 Hours together in September 1948 and he was now convinced to enter his 166 MM at Le Mans.

Chinetti had done all the driving at the Parisian enduro, Selsdon performing the not-unimportant role of providing the car and watching from the pits. This was to be the blueprint for their 1949 Le Mans assault, for which Chinetti and Selsdon would enter the #22 car as privateers, joined by a second 166 MM (a designation that recognised both cars' pedigree on the Mille Miglia) from J.A. Plisson.

A vast army of spectators arrived for race day, undeterred by a blazing June sun that melted some parts of the freshly laid Tarmac. "With the crowds picnicking all round the course, the loud bands, the scantily-garbed girls in the depots and aircraft arriving at Le Mans airfield, ➲

French President Vincent Auriol arrives at the race, ferried in a Renault. GETTY IMAGES

Ferrari had eased up. Whether he was suitably rested or simply unable to relinquish control any longer, Chinetti climbed back aboard at 5:38am, Lord Selsdon having spent one hour and 12 minutes behind the wheel of his own car. Selsdon's lack of action was apparently put down to him not quite feeling the ticket that weekend, something some have since gone on to suggest was self-inflicted!

Chinetti and Ferrari dominate

The pressure on the leader reduced on Sunday morning when the Flahaut/Simon Delahaye expired, its demise officially confirmed at 10.45am. This was just as well for Chinetti, who lost 30 minutes to extensive work on the engine and was suffering from a badly slipping clutch. In another stroke of fortune for the Italian, his main rival – the Delage D6S-3L shared by Henri Louveau and Juan Jover – also had problems, attrition now becoming a major feature of the race. Louveau pushed on, clawing back two laps on the Ferrari, but Chinetti had the nous to bring his car home. He won by a

all the ingredients of a first-class Continental motor-race were present in full measure," said a contemporary report. The race set off at 4pm, ending a 10-year hiatus at the Circuit de la Sarthe, and for the early phase the French reigned supreme. Ecurie Charles Pozzi had entered a pair of new 4.5-litre Delahaye 175S, the #3 machine shared by Pozzi and 1938 race winner Eugène Chaboud and the #4 comprising André Simon and Pierre Flahaut. They ran in this order during the opening stages, while the two Ferraris emerged from the pack to keep a watching brief. It stayed as such into the evening hours, the leading Delahaye pulling more than two laps clear of the Chinetti-driven Ferrari in third. Then, as night approached, the race came to life.

Chinetti was first to hit trouble. He lost almost eight minutes in the pits, returning to the track just as the other Ferrari of Pierre Louis-Dreyfus swept past. There were worse problems for Flahaut in the second-placed Delahaye, which lost nearly 45 minutes to an engine issue. Then, to complete a top-three sweep, the leading Delahaye caught fire on the Mulsanne. Pozzi coaxed the stricken car back to the pits – doing so at dusk without lights, the cause of the fire being electrical – but the game was all but up for the early pacesetter. So, at 9pm, Dreyfus led in his Ferrari – the Flahaut/Simon-driven Delahaye back in second and Chinetti now third.

The curse of the leaders continued when Dreyfus crashed and rolled at Maison Blanche. Darkness was falling and it was suggested that the Ferrari driver may have misjudged an overtake, though he was at least able to scramble free uninjured. Paul Vallée now led at the wheel of a Talbot-Lago, but Chinetti's Ferrari was pressing hard and by 11pm, the Italian had moved into the lead. His two closest challengers retired during the following hours, and by 2am Chinetti led by a lap.

It bears repeating that the 47-year-old Chinetti had been at the wheel from the start, driving from day into night and through early Sunday morning. He passed the 12-hour mark before finally handing the car to Selsdon at 4.26am. When the next hour was complete, the Ferrari was two laps clear, though the Flahaut/Simon-driven Delahaye had risen from the dead and was lapping very rapidly, whereas the

Chinetti at the wheel of the Ferrari 166 MM he helped take to victory. And by 'helped' we mean he drove for over 22 hours. GETTY IMAGES

Enzo Ferrari didn't expect his 166 MM to actually finish, but Chinetti made certain of it, despite a myriad of issues. GETTY IMAGES

The rebuilt pits complex was a big bonus for the Circuit de la Sarthe. This is the view of it from 1950. GETTY IMAGES

little over a lap from the Delage, with the Frazer Nash 2-litre of Harold John Aldington and Norman Culpan third. Newly-elected French president Vincent Auriol was there for the finish, greeting Chinetti as the event's second three-time winner after Woolf Barnato.

There was, however, a sad afterword to what had otherwise been a spectacular return to competition at La Sarthe. At little after 1pm on Sunday afternoon, the Aston Martin DB2 driven by Franco-British racer Pierre Maréchal crashed and overturned at Maison Blanche. The car had been closing in on third place when it suffered a complete brake failure. On Tuesday morning *The Times* newspaper ran an update from the Reuters news agency announcing that the Cheltenham-based racer had died.

For Ferrari, this was the start of a glorious era in sportscar racing. Enzo's cars came to dominate at Le Mans, winning eight times between 1954 and 1965. It also began a special relationship between Ferrari and Chinetti, who became the exclusive US dealer for Enzo's cars, opening a vital market at a time when European economies were still recovering from the war. This has led some to suggest that, without Chinetti, the Italian marque would not have survived its early years.

Chinetti also went on to form the North American Racing Team – better known as NART – which regularly campaigned cars at Le Mans. In 1965 Chinetti won again – this time as a team owner – when his 250 LM driven by Jochen Rindt and Masten Gregory triumphed. More than half a century later, this remains the most recent overall win for a Ferrari at Le Mans. So, until one of the Maranello marque's new Hypercars conquers the race, Luigi Chinetti will continue to bookend Ferrari's success at the Le Mans 24 Hours. ●

Luigi Chinetti and Lord Selsdon celebrate 'their' win, although Selsdon barely broke a sweat. GETTY IMAGES

BLAZING A TRAIL
FEMALE PIONEERS AT LE MANS

Motor racing is one of the few elite sports in which men and women can compete together at the highest level. The Le Mans 24 Hours is no exception. Female participation stretches back to 1930 and continues in 2023, with at least five women set to be on the grid for the centenary race. By Jim Weeks.

While female competitors have a long history at La Sarthe, it has rarely been a simple journey. Women were banned from the event between 1956 and 1971, while several editions have simply featured no female drivers. It would take a book to tell everyone's story, but these are a few of the female pioneers who have blazed a trail the Le Mans 24 Hours.

ODETTE SIKO

This discussion can only begin with Odette Siko. The Parisian shares the distinction of being the first woman to contest the Le Mans 24 Hours, doing so in 1930 alongside Marguerite Mareuse in a Bugatti Type 40. They came home seventh overall to set what is still the record finish for an all-female crew.

Siko made yet more history in 1932 when she shared an Alfa Romeo with Louis Charaval. They placed fourth overall, which remains the best finish for a woman at La Sarthe. She made one more Le Mans start in 1933 but failed to see the chequered flag and did not return as a competitor.

Siko wasn't done behind the wheel, however. Her racing career would span the thirties and garnered praise for performances in speed trials and rallying. Her time in the sport was brought to an abrupt end by World War Two and there is no record of her resuming competition once the conflict was over. Nevertheless, her status as a Le Mans is pioneer is without question.

MARIE-CLAUDE BEAUMONT

The significance of Marie-Claude Beaumont begins with the tragedy of Annie Bousquet. A brave and talented racer, Bousquet lost her life in a sportscar race at Reims in 1956. In response, the powers that be made the bizarre decision to ban women from competing in the Le Mans 24 Hours.

It would take until 1971 for that ban to be lifted – and the woman who broke through was Marie-Claude Beaumont. Motorsport was in her blood: her father was a rally mechanic and occasional competitor and she soon joined in. After a few years of rallying, she went circuit racing and Henri Greder pushed for her to be allowed to compete at Le Mans.

The ACO relented and Beaumont went on to make six starts in the event, winning her class in

Odette Siko (left) still holds the record for the best Le Mans finish for a feamle driver: fourth in 1932 alongside Louis Charaval (right). NEWSPRESS

Marie-Claude Beaumont led the resurgence of female racers at Le Mans. GETTY

Vanina Ickx with her illustrious father, Jacky. GETTY

1974 – an achievement matched the following year by a young Michéle Mouton. Not just a talented driver, she is emblematic of women's return to Le Mans after a 20-year hiatus.

ANNY-CHARLOTTE VERNEY
In terms of starts, no-one has topped Anny-Charlotte Verney. Born into the Le Mans 24 Hours – her grandfather was among the original instigators of the event, while her father was a vice-president of the Automobile Club de l'Ouest – it was no surprise when Anny-Charlotte got behind the wheel and started competing.

After cutting her teeth in rallying, she switched to sports cars and made her Le Mans debut in 1974, kicking off a run of 10 consecutive participations and earning a best overall finish of sixth overall in 1981. Verney was also a class winner in 1978, driving a Porsche 911 Carrera RSR, and scored class podiums on four other occasions.

She later became known as the unfortunate driver paired with unprepared navigator Mark Thatcher on the Paris-Dakar Rally. When they became lost in the desert, it very nearly cost them their lives – and almost caused a diplomatic incident.

VANINA ICKX
As the daughter of a six-time winner, Vanina Ickx was Le Mans royalty before she'd even climbed aboard a car. Having Jacky Ickx for a dad presumably opened a few doors at La Sarthe, but once she'd broken through, Vanina more than earned her place on the grid.

Ickx got her break in 2001 and went on to amass seven starts over the next decade. On a number of those occasions, she was the only woman on the grid, meaning she had the hopes of an entire gender (as well as the Ickx Le Mans legacy) resting on her shoulders.

Her last outing came in 2011 as part of a Belgian super-team alongside Bas Leinders and Maxime Martin. They finished seventh overall,

tying Ickx as the third-best female finisher at Le Mans behind only Siko and Verney.

LEENA GADE
Leena Gade has never driven a competitive lap at Le Mans, yet her status as a pioneer is without question. Joining Audi Sport in 2007, she soon rose to the rank of race engineer and in 2011 led the trio of Lotterer/Tréluyer/Fässler to victory, becoming the first woman to win the event in this capacity. This truly was a magic combination of engineer and drivers, yielding two more wins in 2012 and 2014.

Leena Gade was the first female race engineer to conquer Le Mans. AUDI SPORT

Gade is by no means the only woman to play an important behind-the-scenes role at Le Mans. Today, female engineers and mechanics have become increasingly common, while women have long held crucial management roles in the sport. She is, then, emblematic of their achievements, which often go unnoticed as the drivers take centre stage.

A BRIGHT FUTURE
There were no women on the Le Mans grid in 2015, but female participation has increased considerably since, helped by teams such as Iron Dames and Richard Mille Racing running women-only crews. This has expanded the talent pool and there are several youngsters on the cusp of big things, most notably Lilou Wadoux and Doriane Pin.

Wadoux got her break last year in LMP2 machinery and has since been signed as Ferrari's first-ever female factory driver. Aged 21 and with obvious talent, she will represent the Italian marque's GT squad this year. Pin is yet to make her Le Mans bow, but there is just as much excitement around the 19-year-old, who will drive an LMP2 this year alongside ex-F1 racer Daniil Kvyat and GT legend Mirko Bortolotti. As part of the Iron Dames project, she also has an affiliation with soon-to-be Hypercar entrant Lamborghini.

With ability and youth on their side, Wadoux and Pin are at the vanguard of a new generation of female participation at La Sarthe. Perhaps they can even challenge Odette Siko's record, which has now stood for almost a century. ●

The Iron Dames make history at Spa. Doriane Pin (second from left) will be one to watch for the future. SRO

THE CLASSIC YEARS

With the onset of peace, motorsport could finally get back underway at La Sarthe and with it dawned a new age of technical innovation, giving rise to some of the finest machines and drivers in the history of Le Mans.

The 1950s were a pivotal time for the Le Mans 24 Hours. Now firmly established back on the international sporting calendar, the race experienced a rapid rise in prominence as major manufacturers put down their tooling for weapons of war and began to turn their hands to more traditional fare. In booming post-war economies, road car development was rife – and so was the aggressive advertising that followed the lines of 'speed sells'. Manufacturers quickly cottoned on that if they could make sexy cars that could also win Le Mans, buyers would come calling.

During the 1950s alone, Jaguar, Mercedes-Benz, Ferrari and Aston Martin all went head-to-head, with the challenge of La Sarthe proving not only their product's reliability and

Key Moments

1949   Ferrari's first victory
1951   Porsche's Le Mans debut with the 356
1952   Pierre Levegh's solo attempt ends after 23 hours
1955   The Le Mans disaster. Circuit safety upgrades take place for 1956
1962   Final victory for a front-engined car, the Ferrari 330
1965   Ferrari's last outright Le Mans victory
1966   Ford breaks though, GT40's race average breaks 200kph for the first time
1968   Political unrest delays the race until September. Ford chicane first added to circuit
1969   Jacky Ickx stages a protest by walking during the traditional running start. Final time this start is used
1972   Graham Hill completes the Triple Crown by winning with Matra
1976   First outright victory for a turbocharged car, the Porsche 936

The traditional Le Mans start in 1962. To the left is the gorgeous Aston Martin DP212 of Richie Ginther/Graham Hill. NEWSPRESS

The Winners

1949
Ferrari 166MM
Lord Selsdon/Luigi Chinetti
3178km

1950
Talbot-Lago T26 GS
Louis Rosier/Jean-Louis
Rosier
3465km

1951
Jaguar XK120C
Peter Walker/Peter
Whitehead
3611km

1952
Mercedes-Benz 300SL
(W194)
Hermann Lang/Fritz Riess
3734km

1953
Jaguar C-type
Tony Rolt/Duncan Hamilton
4088km

1954
Ferrari 375 Plus
José Froilán González/
Maurice Trintignant
4061km

1955
Jaguar D-type
Mike Hawthorn/Ivor Bueb
4135km

1956
Jaguar D-type
Ninian Sanderson/Ron
Flockhart
4035km

1957
Jaguar D-type
Ron Flockhart/Ivor Bueb
4397km

1958
Ferrari 250 TR58
Olivier Gendebien/Phil Hill
4102km

1959
Aston Martin DBR1/300
Roy Salvadori/Carroll
Shelby
4348km

1960
Ferrari 250 TR59/60
Paul Frère/Olivier
Gendebien
4218km

1961
Ferrari 250 TR61
Olivier Gendebien/
Phil Hill
4477km

1962
Ferrari 330 LM Spyder
Olivier Gendebien/
Phil Hill
4451km

1963
Ferrari 250P
Lorenzo Bandini/
Lodovico
Scarfiotti
4562km

1964
Ferrari 275P
Jean Guichet/Nino
Vaccarella
4695km

1965
Ferrari 250LM
Masten Gregory/
Jochen Rindt
4677km

1966
Ford MkII
Chris Amon/Bruce
McLaren
4843km

1967
Ford MkIV
Dan Gurney/
AJ Foyt
5233km

1968
Ford GT40
Pedro Rodríguez/
Lucien Bianchi
4453km

1969
Ford GT40
Jacky Ickx/Jackie
Oliver
4998km

1970
Porsche 917K
Hans Herrmann/Richard
Attwood
4608km

1971
Porsche 917K
Helmut Marko/Gijs van
Lennep
5335km

1972
Matra-Simca MS670
Henri Pescarolo/Graham
Hill
4691km

1973
Matra-Simca MS670B
Henri Pescarolo/
Gérard Larrousse
4854km

1974
Matra-Simca MS670B
Henri Pescarolo/
Gérard Larrousse
4607km

1975
Mirage GR8
Derek Bell/
Jacky Ickx
4596km

1976
Porsche 936
Jacky Ickx/Gijs van
Lennep
4770km

1977
Porsche 936/77
Jürgen Barth/Hurley
Haywood/Jacky Ickx
4672km

1978
Renault Alpine A442B
Didier Pironi/Jean-Pierre
Jaussaud
5045km

1979
Porsche 935 K3
Klaus Ludwig/Don
Whittington/Bill
Whittington
4174km

performance, but also its sporting pedigree. Le Mans grids moved further and further from their production car roots and into the first real realms of bespoke sports-racing prototypes. Top speeds would soar to as much as 180mph by the end of the decade.

Ferrari claimed victory in 1949 with the essentially pre-war 166MM, with Talbot-Lago then wheeling out what was in effect a two-seater grand prix car in the form of the Grand Sport T26 to claim 1950's laurels. But the wave of new and improved prototypes was breaking and soon brands such as Bentley, Delahaye and Talbot-Lago itself would be washed away, some never to return.

Jaguar made by far the biggest wave with first its XK-120C of 1951 and resulting C- and D-types, which turned race engineering on its head. Using what was essentially aerospace technology, Coventry firmly got the jump on Maranello and post-war Stuttgart to rack up five wins across a decade that would be punctuated by a disaster that shook the world.

Mercedes-Benz finally made its breakthrough with the 300 SL W194 driven by Hermann

Lang and Fritz Riess in 1952, some 22 years after its last, failed, attempt with the SSK of 1930. And Mercedes chose perhaps the finest time to do so, with multiple works efforts flocking to the event to showcase their latest designs. The 1952 race was notable both for a dozen factory teams from brands such as Lancia, Healey, Aston Martin, Porsche, Fraser-Nash, Renault, Ferrari, Jaguar, the American

Briggs Cunningham and more turning up to take on Mercedes-Benz.

While the German cars would prove superior, finishing one-two, they were very nearly defeated by a heroic attempt from Pierre Levegh, who attempted to drive his Talbot-Lago solo for the entire race. While Briton Eddie Hall is officially the onl driver ever to finish the race solo (1950) his efforts are largely forgotten against that of ➲

The twin Mercedes-Benz 300 SLs cross the line in formation to score the brand's first Le Mans win in 1952. GETTY IMAGES

Levegh, who drove for 23 hours and was leading comfortably before a connecting rod broke. Levegh had been racing without a working rev counter, so some believe a missed gear through exhaustion cost him dearly, others that an engine issue caused the fault. Either way Levegh came agonisingly close to a solo win.

Duncan Hamilton/Tony Rolt outlasted the sister car of Stirling Moss/Peter Walker to score the Jaguar C-type's first victory in 1953, before Ferrari struck back a year later, pairing grand prix aces José Froilán González and Maurice Trintignant in the brutish 5-litre V12 375 Plus.

The race that shook the world

The entire world was shaken by the tragic events on the 1955 race, during which an estimated 80 spectators lost their lives, with over 170 more injured when Pierre Levegh's Mercedes-Benz crashed horrifically during the early evening.

Around four hours into the race, Levegh's 300SLR clipped the rear of British driver Lance Macklin's Austin-Healey at around 150mph, causing the car to become airborne and cartwheel into the earth bank in front of the spectator area, the force of the impact ripping it to shreds and sending many of its heavier components flying into the public area. Its engine and suspension were later found scattered some 100 metres from the track. Levegh was killed on impact and scores of spectators succumbed to the deadly debris.

With emergency services scrambled, the decision was made to allow the race to continue, fearing thousands of swarming spectators would block the local roads for ambulances and medical crews attending the scene.

Mercedes-Benz ordered its remaining cars to retire and the team would withdraw from

motor racing with immediate effect, not to return for 33 years. Jaguar's C-type driven by Mike Hawthorn and Ivor Bueb would go on to win the race, albeit with muted celebration. An official enquiry concluded that no one driver had been at fault, as it was thought that Macklin had been forced to swerve into Levegh's path to avoid Hawthorn slowing to enter the pits unexpectedly.

The following two rounds of the World Sports Car Championship were cancelled and several countries halted motor racing entirely – most famously Switzerland, which only lifted its ban on road-racing events in 2022, some 67 years after the accident. The French

government temporarily halted racing while new safety rules could be formulated.

The ACO reacted by commissioning sweeping changes to the Circuit de la Sarthe, including the demolition of both the pit complex and grandstand in order to widen the track by as much as 13 metres, creating a pit entry lane and increasing the safety area for spectators. The Dunlop Curve was reprofiled with other areas of the circuit such as Maison Blanche, Indianapolis and Arnage also being widened and resurfaced. The changes shortened the lap by about 31 metres and also limited the number of starters from

Porsche made its Le Mans debut in 1951, running the 356, complete with aerodynamic wheel spats. PORSCHE AG

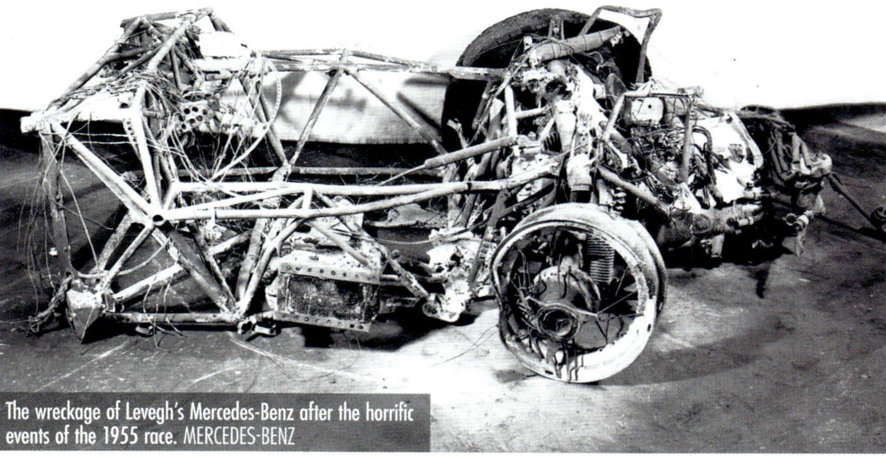

The wreckage of Levegh's Mercedes-Benz after the horrific events of the 1955 race. MERCEDES-BENZ

60 to 52 according to the number of new pit garages available. New rules were also brought in to tackle the rising speeds of the cars. Prototypes were now limited to engines no bigger than 2.5-litres, while full-width windscreens became mandatory and any 'production' car entry had to be backed up by at least 50 units produced. Drivers were also limited to a maximum drive time of 72 consecutive laps and 14 hours total across the race distance.

Jaguar and Ferrari would continue to trade victories, until Aston Martin closed out the decade with its finest sporting achievement to date when Roy Salvadori and Carroll Shelby won aboard the gorgeous DBR1/300, ahead of the sister car of Trintignant/Paul Frère.

Ferrari faces off with Ford

If Jaguar ruled the 1950s, Ferrari would be in a class of its own during the following decade. So much so that the record books still show the Maranello marque as the third most successful in the race's history, despite the fact it hasn't been in a position to challenge for another outright win for the last 50 years.

New rules designed to promote the use of GT cars arrived in the late 1950s, just in time to hail a string of stunning Ferraris. The rules suited the Italian marque perfectly, for Enzo's heart always truly resided with his sports-racers.

This was an age that gave us some of the most beautiful racing cars in history, such as the 250 and its Gioacchino Colombo-designed 3.0-litre V12. Against rather thin opposition, Ferrari walked the early years, racking up seven victories from eight races between 1958 and 1965, until a whole new challenge arrived.

The battle for supremacy between Ferrari and an embittered Henry Ford II is the stuff of Le Mans legend. Famously enraged by Enzo's decision to send his negotiators packing at the last moment when Ford attempted to buy Ferrari in 1963, Ford essentially wrote a blank cheque to create the GT40 for 1964 to try and beat Ferrari at its own game and secure an all-American victory at Le Mans. In truth, the early cars were hopeless, with all three entries that year retiring early before Ford recruited Carroll Shelby to try and turn the GT40 into a winner.

In a story now immortalised through the Hollywood adaptation Le Mans 66 (or Ford v Ferrari, if you weren't in the UK) the car was gradually adapted to accept a hulking 7.0-litre V8 and finely balanced thanks to the efforts of the previously unsung hero, test driver Ken Miles.

Ford dominated Ferrari in 1966, but also shot itself in the foot in the finest fashion when the runaway leader Miles and team-mate Denny Hulme were ordered to slow up to facilitate a photo finish with the second- and third-placed cars of Bruce McLaren/Chris Amon and Ronnie Bucknum/Dick Hutcherson.

Only Ford's top brass hadn't read the rulebook. All three cars crossed the line together, but McLaren and Amon were gifted the victory as they'd started the race 60 feet behind the Miles/Hulme car and had therefore completed the highest distance across the race. Miles was seething on the second step of the podium for a race he rightly should have won.

Ford's GT40 would be the class act from then on, scoring a quartet of wins before a whole new era beckoned and it would be one that would take speed and power to another level.

The accident sent shockwaves through the sport and was pivotal in a new push to improve safety. GETTY IMAGES

The race start in 1955. MERCEDES-BENZ

The seventies stampede

Rules are a huge part of motor racing, but so are the loopholes they can create. Engineers are constantly looking into grey areas or miswording trying to find that extra edge on their opponents, something the great Roger Penske termed as 'the unfair advantage'. And few knew how to exploit the regulations quite like Porsche.

In an attempt to cap the rising the speed of sportscars, the rules were changed to limit prototypes to 3.0-litre engines from 1968. This acted to phase out cars like the GT40 and prompted the Ferrari factory team to walk away after the 512 was regulated out. While it would return for one hit with the 312B prototype in 1973, Ferrari would abandon Le Mans prototypes for the next five decades, choosing to focus on F1 instead.

As you will read further on, the birth of the 917 in 1968 was far from straightforward.

Rushed into life to take advantage of a new homologation rule that allowed 5.0-litre cars to compete if just 25 units were built rather than 50, the 917 was a massive gamble. But it paid off handsomely when the initially unruly machine came good in 1970, with Richard Attwood and Hans Herrmann claiming the manufacturer's first victory at La Sarthe in one of the wettest races on record.

Porsche would win again the following year, with Helmut Marko and Gijs van Lennep triumphing aboard the originally unfancied magnesium, gas-pressured chassis. But a new rival was gaining a head of steam in the form of French manufacturer Matra.

The rise of brands like Jaguar, Ferrari and Porsche meant the wait for a home-grown victory at Le Mans stretched to 22 years by 1972 and Matra was keen to end that. So keen in fact that it scrapped its entire Formula 1 programme to focus on nothing but winning Le Mans.

Having effectively sacked local legend Henri Pescarolo at the end of 1970, Matra offered an olive branch when it expanded to run three cars for an all-out assault on Le Mans in 1972. The only condition was that the then 23-year-old Pescarolo would have to share with 43-year-old two-time F1 world champion Graham Hill.

"Originally, I said 'no way… I will not share with that old man! He will be slow," said Pescarolo. "I was worried about him being able to see in the dark and keep up the pace. But how wrong I was."

By accepting the deal, Pescarolo got a front-row seat to history as he and Hill steamed to victory by 11 laps, in doing so making Hill

Ferrari came to the fore in the early 1960s, thanks to the help of Belgian ace Olivier Gendebien, who would be the first driver to win Le Mans four times. This is his 1962 Ferrari 330. NEWSPRESS

Aston Martin secured its shining moment in 1959, with Roy Salvadori/Carroll Shelby winning in the wonderful DBR1. Here Stirling Moss feeds Salvadori with champagne. ASTON MARTIN RACING

firm began to plant itself firmly at the top of international sportscar racing once again.

While Alpine-Renault (correctly, not Renault-Alpine) briefly interrupted the Stuttgart steamroller when Porsche faltered in 1978, the German brand returned to winning ways a year later in 1979 by essentially beating itself.

With little in the way of factory opposition, Porsche's 936s faced a straightforward run, but both failed to finish, opening the door for a car from the lower GT-based class to win. Funnily enough, that was also a Porsche, as Kremer Racing's 935 K3 driven by Klaus Ludwig and the Whittington brothers, Bill and Don, swept home in a race of attrition. Even then, the winning car lost over an hour parked on the Mulsanne getting makeshift repairs to a snapped drivebelt. But the tone was set for the next decade, it didn't matter what category of car won, chances were it would be a Porsche. ●

the first, and so far only, driver to win motor racing's Triple Crown of the Monaco Grand Prix, Indy 500 and Le Mans.

That success would be the start of great things for both Matra and Pescarolo. Matra would record a hat-trick of victories and Pescarolo would eventually win four times and make a total of 33 Le Mans starts between 1968-1999 to become the most prolific driver in the race's history. Mirage became the first independent constructor to win Le Mans post-war with its Cosworth-powered GR8 in 1975 before the game again changed.

Turbocharging would arrive from 1974. Porsche's 2.1-litre 911 Carrera RSR was the first turbo car to take a class win, ahead of the 936 Spyder becoming the first 'blown' car to secure an outright victory with Jacky Ickx and van Lennep at the wheel in 1976 as the German

Derek Bell and Jacky Ickx made history in 1975, with their Gulf-Mirage becoming the first independent constructor to win the 24 Hours post-war. NEWSPRESS

Ford's famous faux pas. Bruce McLaren/Chris Amon's GT40 crosses the line in 1966 with the car of Ken Miles/Denny Hulme, which had led comfortably but lost the win on a technicality. NEWSPRESS

THE EVOLUTION OF
JAGUAR

What began as a tentative toe-in-the-water exercise in the hands of privateers soon snowballed into a full-on factory attack in the 1950s that produced one of the most successful Le Mans winning streaks ever. This is the story of when Jaguar ruled the world…

Coventry may not sound as sexy as Maranello, but Jaguar's formative factories had a whole lot of history sewn into their walls. The racing programme was born at Swallow Road before then switching to the long-term base at Browns Lane. And it was from this former World War Two shadow factory that the British marque took on and beat the world's best at the Le Mans 24 Hours.

The competition cars that rolled out of Jaguar's doors have gone on to become legendary. The XK120 was the spark for an ever-increasing competitive fire within the company. Then came the C-type, the first true British racing prototype that used aerospace technology to soar above its competition.

And then finally there was the befinned D-type, a precision instrument bringing together the best of both its predecessors to secure a historic hat-trick that helped put Jaguar on top of the world. Jaguar's story is also intertwined with the rise of one of the all-time racing greats, Stirling Moss, even if the company so nearly overlooked his prodigious talent during the early days.

Putting the D before the C. Two classic Jaguars lined up.
JAGUAR HERITAGE/NEWSPRESS

The first win in 1951, taken with an 'unofficial' works XK120 with Peters Walker and Whitehead. JAGUAR HERITAGE/NEWSPRESS

120mph. While the majority of XK120s were shipped aboard – a useful tactic to help secure additional supplies of such rare materials as Britain's government rewarded international traders post-war – domestic customers soon began to realise the sporting potential of the XK120 – and the factory knew the best way to shift cars was to race them, so willingly helped.

The first racing variant appeared in 1949 during a one-hour production car race in support of the *Daily Express* International Trophy at Silverstone in 1949. Drivers Leslie Johnson and Peter Walker dominated, going on to finish one-two to ram home the idea that Jaguar was on to something.

A year later and Lyons had made his mind up – sort of. The decision was made to prepare three XK120s, ship them off to Le Mans with a trailer-load of parts and then hand them over to privateers, so as to protect the Jaguar name just in case they should be totally out-paced.

They weren't. Two finished the race, but the fastest – handled by Leslie Johnson and Bert Hadley – had run second for a period before eventually retiring with clutch failure after 21 hours. Jaguar's management was satisfied with the base performance, but knew there was more to come. And then a letter landed on Lyons' desk.

Unknown hotshot

During 1950, Stirling Moss was a relatively unknown hotshot. Just 21 and with only a handful of 500cc Formula 3 appearances under his belt, Lyons wasn't minded to hand out one of his new-found racing XKs to a novice, as Moss recalled to journalist Simon Taylor in his book *My Racing Life*.

He said: "Even though my sights were set on Formula 1, I realised the importance of long-distance sports car racing. I tried to convince Jaguar to give me a chance at Le Mans or the Tourist Trophy at Dundrod in Northern Ireland. The TT was a really demanding event, run over 320 miles: 7.4-miles of narrow public roads through hilly country, with fast and slow corners and a long, undulating downhill straight. I contacted Jaguar before the TT but word ➲

But what was the secret to Jaguar's post-war success? Clues lie firmly in the company's early belief in revolution over evolution.

Having founded the Swallow Sidecar Company in 1922 to build passenger sidecars for motorcycles, William Lyons quickly diversified into coachbuilding automobile bodies and the term Jaguar first appeared as a model name on Lyons' first four-wheeled product, the SS 2.5-litre saloon of 1935. When war broke out, the company stopped building cars and instead turned its hand to supporting the air force, turning its trade to building wings, fuel tanks and other components for Whitley bombers.

By 1945, Swallow Car Company officially became Jaguar and car production was back at the top of the agenda, but not just any humdrum cars. Jaguar set out to nail the sports car market and just three years later unveiled the XK120 at the London Motor Show. With a price tag of £1,300 and a promise to be one of the fastest production cars on the planet, it was an instant hit.

The name derives from the twin-overhead cam 3.4-litre XK engine and Jaguar's estimation that the slippery shape of the aluminium bodywork could help it achieve at top speed of

Turning the tide at Reims in 1953, when Moss would win with disc brakes – a world first. JAGUAR HERITAGE/NEWSPRESS

The Jaguar team lined up in the pits in 1953. JAGUAR HERITAGE/NEWSPRESS

Duncan Hamilton and Tony Rolt celebrate their record-breaking win, the first Le Mans victors to average over 100mph. JAGUAR HERITAGE/NEWSPRESS

came back that [Jaguar racing manager] Lofty England, while he accepted I'd shown speed in F3, I was too inexperienced to be entrusted with one of their cars. The implication being that I would probably crash, bringing Jaguar unwelcome publicity."

Turned down but not turned off, Moss was instead handed a drive in a private XK120, owned by journalist and racer Tommy Wisdom, and Moss didn't waste his chance. Jaguar's factory team entered cars for Peter Whitehead and Johnson, but they were powerless to prevent the young Moss from snatching pole and then driving off into the distance after taking a single lap to acclimatise himself to both car and track.

By the finish, Moss was three miles clear and a message had been sent. It didn't take Lyons long to pick this one up either and he promptly signed Moss to a works contract for 1951 during the post-race party.

With a driver like Moss onboard, Jaguar now needed a car capable of doing the job. That arrived in the shape of the XK120C, the C standing for Competition, which eventually just

became regarded as the C-type Jaguar. The first design was aimed specifically at Le Mans.

In order to create the C-type, Jaguar essentially started from scratch. Preserving the running gear from the original XK120, the C-type would be based around an all-new frame designed by chief engineer William Haynes. Gone was the ash wood underpinning on the first car, replaced by a lightweight tubular structure and draped in an all-new, curvaceous

aluminium body jointly developed by Heynes, Bob Knight and Malcolm Sayer, who would become a key appointment after starting work at the company in early 1951.

An aircraft engineer by trade, Sayer brought a new way of thinking to automobile aerodynamics. He understood that by making things light and effectively knocking the slab-shaped corners off, cars could greatly increase performance by lowering drag. And that was a key part of the C-type's success.

With its sculpted front end, long flowing bonnet and rear end that tucked away to the ground behind the driver, the C-type was a new kind of slippery. The XK engine was retained and during the C-type's first iteration ran with SU carburettors to produce around 205bhp, plus drum brakes.

Jaguar entered three works cars for the C-type's Le Mans debut in 1951, driven by Peters Walker and Whitehead, Moss and Jack Fairman and Leslie Johnson/Clemente Biondetti.

Class of the field

The cars immediately proved the class of the field, pulling some 150mph along the Mulsanne and out-pacing even the fancied Talbot-Lagos, which were not much more than two-seater grand prix cars. Moss was sent out as pace-setter for the race, ordered by Lofty England to hare away in an attempt to force the rival Ferraris and Talbots to run at an unsustainable pace, therefore breaking the opposition.

Moss did so at a tremendous rate, lowering the lap record, and was a full lap clear of the field by the end of his first 3.5-hour stint. The C-types ran one-two-three after four hours, but problems soon crept in. First the Johnson/Biondetti car stopped with a loss of oil pressure and then just after midnight Moss crawled to a halt on the Mulsanne with a similar issue. Post-race investigation would reveal that a copper oil pipe had vibrated loose on both cars.

Regardless, the sole remaining C-type of Whitehead and Walker ran like clockwork, greeting the dawn with a nine-lap lead that it would hold to the flag. Jaguar's C-type had won at its very first attempt.

But there would be no successful defence the following year. May's Mille Miglia road race showed the C-types to be considerably down on straight-line speed against renewed competition from Ferrari and the new 300 SL from Mercedes-Benz. Fearing a battering at Le Mans, Jaguar rushed into a redesign of the C-type's front end, lengthening the nose and tail sections in an attempt to reduce drag even further and allow the car to pierce through the air at high speed. These changes also necessitated a redesign of the cooling system and the two tweaks would go on to have disastrous

A cutaway of the C-type's chassis. JAGUAR HERITAGE/NEWSPRESS

Rolt/Hamilton's car takes the finish in 1953. Note the smashed windscreen due to a bird strike. JAGUAR HERITAGE/NEWSPRESS

the three reworked cars for Le Mans in 1953. And despite the race featuring a raft of factory entries from brands like Aston Martin, Alfa Romeo, Talbot-Lago, Lancia and Cunningham, Jaguar and Ferrari were a cut above and went head-to-head for the win.

All three C-types ran under the lap record in practice and once again, Moss led the early stages of the race. But once again he would be undone by misfortune as a misfire struck just 20 laps in. He made an extra stop and a clogged fuel filter was diagnosed and cured, but the car was dropped well down the order by the time it eventually rejoined.

Lapping above 100mph consistently, Rolt/ Hamilton's C-type edged out a lead over the Ferraris and Cunninghams, despite its windscreen being smashed by a bird strike, leading to both drivers receiving a real beating from the wind.

consequences as all three works cars retired from overheating within the first four hours.

There would be some light relief from the year though, as Moss was handed a C-type to race in the Reims Grand Prix just a week later. Moss persuaded Jaguar's engineers to rip out the drum brakes and fit a Dunlop disc system. He would go on to record the first-ever race win for a car running disc brakes that very weekend.

Mistakes noted, Jaguar went back to the drawing board again for 1953. Firstly the chassis was constructed from a thinner-gauge tubing to trim additional weight, steel fuel tanks were replaced with rubber bags, the XK engine now breathed through triple choke Weber carbs to produce 220bhp and underneath it all lay those Dunlop disc brakes. It proved the perfect blend and make for a record-breaking Le Mans weekend.

Moss/Walker, Whitehead/Ian Stewart and Tony Rolt/Duncan Hamilton occupied

Mood-D. The D-type is one of the best-looking cars of the era. JAGUAR HERITAGE/NEWSPRESS

A C- and D-type from the rear. The D's rear fin aided aerodynamic stability. JAGUAR HERITAGE/NEWSPRESS

Ecurie Ecosse flew the flag after Jaguar withdrew, winning in 1956 and 1957. This is Flockhart/Bueb in '57. JAGUAR HERITAGE/NEWSPRESS

The rampant pace took its toll and when the Ferrari's clutch gave in and the Cunningham's mighty V8 began to fade, Jaguar was in the box seat. Rolt/Hamilton won by four laps, with Moss/Walker putting in a superb drive to snatch second from the American machine. All three C-types finished, in first, second and fourth, setting a new mileage record for the race, and also becoming the first machines to win at an average of over 100mph (105.5mph). Jaguar was in the record books for all the right reasons, and its sales figures reflected the achievement nicely.

Birth of the D-type

However, with the C-type hitting its limit of development, and Ferrari et al already focusing on its next-generation cars, Jaguar needed another clean slate to continue its streak. It arrived in the form of the ground-breaking 1954 D-type.

Just three years on from its spaceframe construction, Jaguar already believed a monocoque chassis was the future, so Haynes and Sayer together penned a revolutionary elliptical tub, with no corners whatsoever to its outsides. Constructed from sheets of aluminium, argon arc-welded together for both strength and weight saving. To the tub was welded (or bolted on later versions) the front and rear assemblies and the XK engine, which now used a dry-sump oil system allowing the unit to be mounted lower in the car, both decreasing the frontal area and lowering the D-type's centre of gravity. Sayer then clad the lot in beautifully sleek bodywork and wrap-around windscreen, together with the distinctive rear fin to aid stability at high speeds.

Three cars turned out for Le Mans in 1954, but it proved a false dawn as all three lost time with fuel filter problems, one had a transmission go and Moss would again be set back when the braking system gave up. It would be the final Le Mans for Moss as a Jaguar driver, and perhaps the greatest driver never to win the F1 World Championship would also never win Le Mans.

"Le Mans was never a lucky race for me," recalled Moss in *My Racing Life*. "My three races in a D-type all ended in retirement: at Reims a half-shaft broke and in the TT a piston failed. That's why I look back on the C-type with much more affection… especially the lighter C-types with disc brakes in 1953, which gave us a great advantage, particularly at the end of the Mulsanne. While the D- had been much faster than the C- on wide open spaces like Le Mans, it never felt at home somewhere like Dundrod."

Rolt aboard the first D-type in the Le Mans pits in 1954. JAGUAR HERITAGE/NEWSPRESS

The 1956 Ecurie Ecosse winner in the pit. Considered the most complete D-type in the world to this day, it sold in 2016 for £16.6m. JAGUAR HERITAGE/NEWSPRESS

A race of all shapes and sizes. The diminutive D-type against a hulking XK140 in 1956. JAGUAR HERITAGE/NEWSPRESS

With problems ironed out a year later, the D-type would make its breakthrough under sombre circumstances, Mike Hawthorn and Ivor Bueb's factory car beating Aston Martin DB3s in a race forever overshadowed by the tragedy that claimed the lives of so many spectators and Mercedes-Benz driver Pierre Levegh. Mercedes withdrew it team mid-race and wouldn't return for more than 30 years.

Ecurie Ecosse takes over

When new production rules were brought in for 1956, Jaguar managed to persuade the ACO that the D-type qualified due to the rising number of customer cars the company was building, so the team returned the following year with some key tweaks. The cars were now 130kg lighter and boasted 285bhp, helped by the addition of fuel injection.

But the works ranks were thinned when Paul Frère spun his D-type right in the path

The D-type in silhouette. JAGUAR HERITAGE/NEWSPRESS

of Fairman, causing a multi-car collision that put both out inside the first hour. Hawthorn led in the remaining car, but had to stop with a misfire that was traced to a hairline crack in a fuel line.

It then fell to the customer D-type of Ecurie Ecosse to do the business, with Ninian Sanderson and Ron Flockhart leading the Aston Martin DB3S home by a lap – the car

crewed by Peter Collins and, you guessed it, Moss ... second again.

Realising customer success weighed just as heavy as that of the factory, Jaguar withdrew its works team at the end of the season claiming it had achieved all it wanted. Yet it agreed to continue supporting the likes of Ecurie Ecosse. And the works quit at precisely the wrong time, as the following year proved to be the D-type's crowning glory. With its engine enlarged to 3.8-litres, the D-type proved unstoppable, with Flockhart and Bueb leading home a Jaguar whitewash as D-types finished first-fourth, with a private entry from Duncan Hamilton/Masten Gregory making it five inside the top six.

New rules for 1958 limited engine sizes to just three litres, which effectively spelled the end for both the D-type and Jaguar's golden era at Le Mans. Jaguar did fit a smaller engine, but the D-type never thrived with it, eventually bowing out of the entry altogether after 1960 as Ferrari's 250 model came to the fore.

The glory days were over, but the cars, and the engineering brilliance behind them, would go on to inspire a whole new era at Le Mans. ●

UNCOILING THE COBRA

Back when Le Mans was a simpler affair than it is now, competition cars could also take to the roads. Eric Dymock got his hands on a bona-fide piece of American history.

AC Cobra, 39 PH, as it looks now. You would never guess it had been a Le Mans class winner. ERIC DYMOCK

t seems scarcely believable when looking at the modern race, but there once was a time when competing cars would be driven to the Le Mans 24 Hours, complete the entire event and then be driven home again. Put up against the modern age of cutting-edge multi-million-pound prototypes, that would look as alien on our roads as an actual UFO.

While the early days of Le Mans were very much an Anglo-French battle for honours, the post-war period brought a whole new force into play – the Americans. Suddenly, big-capacity, big-hitters started to make the trip across the Atlantic to compete in the world's biggest endurance race and they brought with them some stunning machinery. The AC Cobra was a classic case in point.

I was working on the road test staff at *The Motor* magazine at the time when a chance meeting with Ninian Sanderson outside Harrods just after Le Mans in 1963 presented a unique opportunity. By then, the Scottish

The Cobra in the pits in 1963. Number 4 alongside was another privately-entered AC Cobra, driven by Ed Hugus and Peter Jopp. It would be disqualified for a premature oil change. AC HERITAGE

car dealer-turned yachtsman and racer was a grizzled veteran of Le Mans and had just completed his ninth attempt at the 24 Hours. Having won it outright in 1956 aboard a works Jaguar D-type, he was finally celebrating another success, a class-winning run in his first American car, the factory AC Cobra.

Knowing him well from Ecurie Ecosse and Glasgow motor trade days, he suggested I approach AC Cars about testing what he had raced in the 24 Hours' alongside Peter Bolton. The AC had already proved impressive, given it had completed the race as one of just a handful of survivors in the over 4,000cc class, winning it at an average of 108mph. And all of this was under the watchful eye of Stirling Moss, who acted as team manager/adviser to the AC Cars team for Le Mans.

Even *to The Motor's* experienced road testers, Cobras were exceptional, particularly a tuned, racing one. The car that had just taken seventh place at Le Mans was brought back from France, had its axle ratio changed and was taken to MIRA (the Motor Industry Research Association) proving ground at Lindley, which we used every week for testing cars for an exciting day's motoring.

The Cobra was basically an AC Ace chassis with a 4.7-litre American Ford V8 engine and Borg Warner gearbox instead of its regular straight six-cylinder engine. The brainchild of legendary tuner Carroll Shelby, who specialised in racing big, exciting sports cars in Europe and the

United States in the late 1950s (he won Le Mans with Roy Salvadori in a DBR1/300 Aston Martin in 1959), the Cobra represented the highest development of the John Tojeiro-designed AC all-independent tubular frame. It was suitably strengthened for the Ford 289 engine producing, with the four double-choke 48/DMI Webers of the Le Mans car, around 330bhp.

With a light alloy body and detachable hardtop, the Le Mans Cobra appeared to be dominated by its wheels, much larger and fatter than regular AC Ace and Acecas. The enormous 6.00-15 front and 7.00-15 rear Dunlop R.6 racing tyres took up the entire wheel arch and bulged out of the sides as well. They were mounted on alloy wheels to accommodate larger-than-standard discs and we drove with the Le Mans pressures of 50lb (3.4bar) all round.

AC Cars anticipated using the car on circuits in the UK and changed the axle ratio from the Le Mans 3.07:1 to 3.77:1 before bringing it to MIRA. Otherwise, it was in exactly the condition in which it had crossed the line at 4pm just 11 days previously. AC said that the oil hadn't even been changed and the front tyres were those with which it started the race. Incredibly, after a full-day's thrashing, they only looked about three-parts worn. But the rears were another matter, having taken a lot of punishment from that muscly V8. But whatever their state at the start, they were much more worn by the end of the afternoon.

Ninian Sanderson and Peter Bolton in action aboard 39 PH at Le Mans in 1963. GETTY IMAGES

The AC Cobra covered 310 laps on its way to seventh overall and the Over-3-Litre GT class victory in 1963. AC HERITAGE

Better furnishings

The inside of the Cobra was much better furnished than most competition GT cars. Carpets were an astonishing luxury (yes, carpets, in a Le Mans car… don't get those now!) and the seats comfortable, but surprisingly the adjustment was inadequate for medium-height drivers to sit at arm's length from the wheel. This was impractical in the Cobra, however, and since the steering was heavy it must have been tiring after a day and a night's driving.

Other constant reminders of the racer character were the huge funnel in the roof behind the driver's head to the 30gal (136.4l) fuel tank and the shattering noise inside at full cry. The facia was a clutter of small dials and you felt that three-quarters of the Mulsanne must have been spent checking water temperature, battery charge, oil pressure, fuel level and engine speed. The standard speedometer was obscured by the large spokes of a splendid, thick-rimmed AC-manufactured, wood-rimmed

Repainted in its red and white livery, 39 PH out on the roads of Scotland. ERIC DYMOCK

steering wheel. It had not been compensated for changes in axle ratio which made it read 150mph for 120mph. Not that the performance needed flattering.

Using 6,400rpm on the clear arc-type tachometer, 40mph could be reached in about three seconds 60 in under five, 80 in 8.1 seconds and 100 in just 12. A further six seconds or so took you past 120mph before the straight gave out and the time for the standing quarter-mile was 11 seconds, with a terminal speed of almost 107mph, still in third gear. On the banked high-speed circuit, the Cobra went through the electronic timing strip at 139.6mph at about 6,200rpm but would gain several hundred more revs before it was necessary to slow down for the next banking and one felt it would easily pull over 6,500rpm on a slightly longer straight, representing about 148mph.

MIRA's electronic time trap on the inner road circuit credited me with 183mph, which felt quick. Alas *The Motor's* technicians pooh-poohed its electronics, their slide rules

The Cobra heads a pack of chasing Ferraris, Alfa Romeos and Aston Martin Zagato and Porsches. It was a good-looking field in 1963. GETTY IMAGES

calculating the change in axle ratio made it more likely about 170mph. On the banked circuit, we managed just short of 140mph, about 22.5mph per 1,000rpm, through another electronic trap, so at 6,500rpm it might have managed 146-147mph. On the Le Mans axle, it was doing 160mph on the Mulsanne at 5,500rpm, or around 29mph per 1,000rpm, so had it been able to pull 6,500rpm with its rather blunt aerodynamics, that would be 189mph.

On the fresh axle ratio, even at 7,000rpm, 165mph at MIRA was more likely than 180mph, so discretion suggested that my 183mph be excluded. MIRA had a second electronic time trap on the road course, on which you could go faster before braking for the next corner. Perhaps the slide-rulers at *The Motor* (usually quite precise) were not being perverse to rob me of my fastest time of the day, but that was assuming, of course, that all their other calculations were correct.

Performance of that sort was still formidable, yet the handling made it unexpectedly easy to cope with. The figures disappointed AC technicians, probably owing to a flat spot around 3,500rpm because of the need for some engine readjustments, but bearing in mind nothing had been touched since completing 2,592 very hard miles at very high speeds it was scarcely surprising. As it was, it would have been fast enough to have won the 1956 race which Sanderson, co-driving with Ron Flockhart, did with an Ecurie Ecosse D-type Jaguar.

On the road circuit at MIRA, the Cobra exhibited a powerful, consistent tendency to run wide on corners but stuck so firmly to the road that on a long bend it was only necessary to turn on a little extra steering lock and a lot of the immense power to set it up in a stable, predictable line. Even tight corners in the lower gears could be taken with a good deal of power on. There was quite a lot of body roll for a competition car, despite the heavy anti-roll bars, but the frame felt stiff and taut, even at high speed on the rather bumpy banking.

The Borg Warner gearbox turned out to be unexpectedly good, enabling rapid changes with powerful synchromesh, but the ratios were rather wide. The short lever needed a firm movement together with a clutch not unduly heavy but took unkindly to a succession of standing starts. Apart from a strong smell of hot lining, however, it did not appear to suffer any permanent issues.

Flat spot

It was a difficult car to get off the line on account of the flat spot in the rev range and one was faced with the choice of letting the clutch in at around 6,000rpm and coping with the tremendous wheelspin, or starting at a lower engine speed and having the revs die momentarily below the all-important 3,500rpm. The large disc brakes, with racing pads and heavy pedal pressures, steadfastly refused to show any signs of fade, even under the stress of stopping the car from over 120mph every two or three minutes while we took acceleration figures.

With an engine looking like Battersea Power station – one upright carburettor choke per cylinder, it consumed fuel at Le Mans at around 8mpg. A spare fan belt was still taped up beside the radiator header tank, just in case its driver should fall foul of a snapped one out on track and need to make swift repairs to stay in the race. The driver had foam padding to the right of the knee to help cope with sideways g-forces on corners.

The Le Mans Cobra was large, powerful and exciting. It had the high-scuttled feel of an earlier era with the stiff-framed precision and comfortable ride of a then-modern thoroughbred. Driving a true road-going Cobra the same day showed that the deep braying exhaust note of the big V8 could be subdued without affecting flexibility and acceleration. It was unobtrusive but immensely swift – not kick-in-the-back style, but more like a rocket leaving the launching pad and going on – and on – and on...

And just like that, our test was over. I would meet PH 39 again in 1990, by which point it had exchanged the light green paint it originally wore for a fresh red with white stripe. It had also gained an extra air intake at the front and the wheels were different, but the jacking points looked much like those it would have had for the 24 Hours' race. Nigel Hulme drove it in the Ecurie Ecosse Historic Motor Tour of Scotland and as I photographed the car on the climb towards Glencoe on Rannoch Moor, I couldn't help but think what fun its driver must have been having. I certainly did. ●

THE BIRTH OF A LEGEND

Ask anybody to name a classic Le Mans racer and chances are the Porsche 917 will feature highly on the agenda. Yet this much-revered classic had far from an easy life.

Porsche's 917 may have transcended the race it was built to conquer and become one of the cult classic racing cars of all time, but it's easy to forget that it also very nearly brought its maker to its knees.

The 917 was a gamble, perhaps the biggest in Porsche's history to date – a car designed to do only one thing, win the Le Mans 24 Hours and propel the brand to the forefront of the sports car market.

Yes, it may have had the added bonus of being immortalised in the 'King of Cool' Steve McQueen's famous movie, *Le Mans*, but the 917 worked its way into the hearts of enthusiasts thanks to more than just the silver screen. The story of its dramatic and troubled birth gives the car a comeback king vibe, while the loophole-exploiting history deepens its intrigue. Being timelessly pretty and having an enviable winning record also helps. Without the 917, Porsche's all-time record of 19 Le Mans victories simply wouldn't have come to fruition. The Stuttgart brand's winning run started with the 917 in 1970 and pretty much every success it has had since can be drawn back in some way to its seminal 917 prototype.

Considering the legacy this 500bhp beast left, its lifespan was relatively brief. The 917 was only raced as an official factory entry for three seasons between its debut in 1969 until its retirement in 1972. During then it contested 21 events and won 14 of them – including two Le Mans victories.

However, while the 917's sole mission was to achieve success at Le Mans, it actually carried with it a huge burden as one of the most expensive and pressured racing projects ever, having gone from drawing board to full-scale production in just a matter of months.

Porsche in the early 1960s wasn't on the sort of financially stable ground it is today. It was a time of transition for the firm, with sales of the ageing 356 road car dropping and its sporting aspirations struggling. Indeed, even its Formula 1 programme was growing increasingly stagnant, with just a single grand prix win in 1962 to show for its development and investment.

Sure enough, Porsche quit F1 at the end of 1963 to fund instead the development of the all-new 911 flagship road model. But even that needed a boost during its early years. And what better way to hike sales than by enhancing the firm's image through motorsport?

Porsche boss Ferdinand Piech – the grandson of marque founder Ferdinand Porsche – was clearly an early adopter of the 'win on a Sunday, sell on a Monday' mantra. And it was the ambitious 26-year-old who effectively green-lighted what would go down as one of the most daring Le Mans programmes in history.

Another piece of the puzzle was engine guru Hans Mezger. Having previously transformed the firm's mediocre F1 engine into a race-winning unit, Mezger had been reassigned to the 911 project after the F1 withdrawal, but it was his spark with Piech that produced a will ➲

An early 917 prototype is rolled out of the factory. PORSCHE AG

Porsche's efforts to build and line-up enough 917s to satisfy homologation rules was near-ruinous. PORSCHE AG

The interior was sparse, and drivers were concerningly far forward. Some even suggested their feet were part of the crash structure. PORSCHE AG

The car made its competition debut at the 1966 Daytona 24 Hours, finishing sixth overall and winning the 2.0-litre class. With Piech now overseeing the production of race cars, 50 examples of the 906 were sold, creating Porsche's first real customer base in international sportscar racing.

Things would ratchet up when the FIA opted to shake up the rulebook in an attempt to undo its own damage – and in doing so, unintentionally opened a loophole that the 917 flew straight through.

In an attempt to cap rising speeds at Le Mans, the FIA's mandate to cap all prototype engines to 3.0-litres for 1968 hadn't gone to plan. Ford's factory had quit after whitewashing Le Mans with its GT40 and Ferrari pulled its entries in protest. All that was left were a few older 5.0-litre Fords and Lolas that were still allowed to run purely because 50 or more examples had been built.

In response to the shrinking entries, the FIA revised the rule for 1969, stating that instead of 50, manufacturers would now only have to create 25 cars to pass homologation and then they could run engines up to 5.0-litres.

That created an opportunity, but not perhaps one Porsche was truly ready for. But its rival was. At the time, Enzo Ferrari had sold most of his road car business to Fiat and had used the funding to commission the build of the 5.0-litre 512 for 1970 as a development of the 1969 312P. With Ferrari threatening to steal Porsche's thunder, the German firm embarked on a seemingly crazy task, taking advantage of the loophole and commissioning the construction of 25 new racing cars in just 10 months. And they'd be fitted with a brand-new 4.5-litre engine to boot.

The investment was huge. Porsche was already busy building and replacing the chassis for its fleet of 908s, which required constant maintenance thanks to the stringent gas-pressure testing of its aluminium spaceframe. Combined with that workload, the development and construction of 25 new cars put the workforce under extreme pressure to meet the FIA's homologation deadline for the 1969 Le Mans 24 Hours. The effort reportedly nearly drove Porsche to bankruptcy.

The first problem was the engine. Porsche assessed expanding its 3.0-litre flat-eight 908 engine, but early examples suffered from extreme vibration from the clutch and

for the firm to go racing again, but in something commercially relevant to the 911. The pair redesigned the road car's 2.0-litre flat-six 'boxer' engine to have the fundamentals of a racing unit. They then oversaw the development of the 904, the first forerunner to the 917.

The 904 was a lightweight, ladder chassis, fibreglass-bodied GT car that soon earned a reputation for being essentially bullet-proof. It secured a one-two on the 1964 Targa Florio, and swept the board in the 2-litre class of the World Sportscar Championship, and in doing so created some much-desired media attention for Piech.

The way forward

He convinced Porsche's board that sports car racing was the way forward, not just to boost the brand, but also to sell the 911 to the public.

Porsche agreed funding to take the project to the next step. A steel spaceframe chassis was constructed and fitted with a race-tuned version of the 911's production engine. The unit had been heavily worked over by Mezger and produced twice the power but weighed the same due to lightweight crank casings and components. This became the Carrera 6, or 906.

The huge rear track of the 917. This is the short-tail or kurzheck version. PORSCHE AG

Richard Attwood takes a glug of water before heading out at Le Mans, 1970. PORSCHE AG

Porsche's band of heroes at the 1969 Targa Florio. L-R: Umberto Maglioli, Richard Attwood, Brian Redman, Ferry Porsche, Hans Herrmann, Udo Schütz, Rolf Stommelen (glasses), Vic Elford, Rudi Lins, Gérard Larrousse and Gerhard Mitter at the wheel of the 908/2. PORSCHE AG

crankshaft and the use of a longer, flatter crank was thought to be too much of a risk. Instead, it ditched the plan and began developing its first 12-cylinder engine. The unit it settled on was a 4.5-litre 180-degree, air-cooled flat-12, manufactured from a steel block but with exotic alloys such as titanium, magnesium and lithium comprising many components to limit weight. Porsche opted for this approach to keep the centre of gravity low in the chassis, whereas a traditional V8 project would have raised it.

Rushed through

The engine was codenamed 'Project 912' and was rushed through design and production, but had input from every one of Porsche's specialists. Ian Bamsey writes in his book *Porsche 917, The Ultimate Weapon*: "Project 912 ran a 10.5.1 compression ratio and was rated close to 550bhp at 8,400rpm. Mezger reflected: "From the start, it was better in its mechanical behaviour than any other Porsche engine before it." He also noted that it ran very dry because of its improved lubrication system. With 25 examples already committed, Piech and Mezger could breathe a well-earned sigh of relief."

The one salvation of Porsche's plan was the chassis. It had achieved notable success with the 908, so why not use that? The 908 had been forged with extensive wind-tunnel testing and

component destruction testing, so should prove a reliable base.

Porsche rushed the 25 917s through build and eventually lined each one up outside the factory, just in time to satisfy the FIA's homologation demands. One car was sent to that year's Le Mans test by the factory Porsche Salzburg team, with Brian Redman as the main driver. But the 917 was beset with issues from the start.

The car proved increasingly unstable at both high speed and under braking. Redman reported having to use the entire width of the Mulsanne to keep the car under control. The issue arose from the aerodynamic plan

Porsche's short-tailed 917 proved the machine to beat in the wet. PORSCHE AG

of the 908 and its suspension settings being incompatible with the new-found power of the 917. Porsche was adamant that the 917 would be faster than anything before it down the straights and engineered the car for this sole purpose. And it was, by about 19mph, but in this trim the sloped long-tail section fitted with slim spoiler taken from the 908 did reduce drag, but also produced lift. Likewise, the lack of cooling channels to the brakes meant that stopping was also a challenge.

Le Mans in 1969 was a disaster. The rushed 917s were beset with aerodynamic problems and proved a real handful. The car enjoyed terrific straight-line speed, if the drivers could hold it straight. Redman once recalled using the full width of the Mulsanne to try and keep a hold on it.

The race was then overshadowed when privateer John Woolfe lost control of his 917 into Maison Blanche and was fatally injured. Both works cars failed to make it through the night with clutch and transmission problems.

Porsche realised it needed help and approached British team JW Automotive and its boss John Wyer. Wyer had been instrumental in helping Ford to Le Mans success with the GT40 and with Ford now gone, JWA took the contract as the official Porsche works team.

The first thing Wyer did was arrange a three-day test at the Osterreichring in the autumn of 1969 in a bid to sort the 917's problems. JWA brought a pair of 917 Coupés and a pair of prototype open-topped 917PA Spyders. Redman, Leo Kinnunen, Kurt Ahrens and Piers Courage were recruited to drive.

The team worked to find a happy compromise between the suspension settings on the two cars. The drivers preferred the setting on the Spyder, which ran lower spring ratios and was therefore less volatile. But by far the largest breakthrough was the aero.

Gnats show the way

When JWA's chief engineer John Horsman looked at the car after the first day of running

The 917 on its way to victory at Le Mans in 1970. It would kick-start Porsche's glorious run of wins at La Sarthe. PORSCHE AG

he realised something. "The entire front end was splattered with dead gnats, yet there were hardly any on the rear spoilers," said Horsman. "I knew the gnats would flow over the bodywork exactly as the air flowed, similar to smoke in a wind tunnel. I knew immediately that we had to raise the rear deck and then attach small adjustable spoilers to the trailing edge. It was obvious that if the whole rear body surface was in the airstream, it would be able to exert downforce."

The team riveted on an extension to the rear bodywork, which raised the dovetail section above and beyond the rear wheel arches. Two near vertical flaps were also added.

Wingrove continued: "Redman went out for a few laps and ended up staying out for many as he grew in confidence with the 917. He returned to the pits beaming, saying: "Now you can *drive* this car!" Porsche was amazed to see its drivers suddenly throwing the 917 around 'like a rally machine'.

Taking the flag to cement the legend. PORSCHE AG

Champagne flies on the podium after victory, 1970.
PORSCHE AG

Additional changes were also made to the front. Two ducting scoops were added inside of each headlight to channel air to the brakes, which were now larger. And the frontal oil cooler intake spouted a front lip to both boost downforce and also suck additional air into the chassis. Porsche also toyed with the idea of installing an engine fan to help suck air out from beneath the car, but abandoned the concept when a test mule repeatedly got clogged with dirt on road tracks.

What Porsche had now was a car that depended much more on aerodynamic downforce instead of outright grunt and one that was geared toward ultimate lap time, not top speed. Back at the factory, Porsche had also increased the size of its engine to 4.9 litres to better rival the incoming Ferraris.

The revised 917 remained in its development cycle for the start of 1970, as Porsche ran its 908 in the opening races at the Nürburgring and the Targa Florio. The 917's sole purpose was to win Le Mans and Porsche wanted it to be ready.

Porsche used the time to develop two different specifications, the short tail (Kurzheck) and a new low-drag Le Mans specific long-tail (Langheck) version.

It entered seven factory-backed 917s at Le Mans, three for JWA, two through Salzburg and two through new partner Martini Racing. There was also a privateer car for David Piper and Gijs van Lennep.

The longtail Salzburg car of Vic Elford/Kurt Ahrens Jr dominated qualifying thanks to its monstrous straight-line speed. Porsche was in good form and stormed into an early lead.

The 917 had a distinct pace advantage over the five works Ferrari 312s, but they had a strategic edge, being able to run two laps longer on their fuel loads. That in itself produced a fascinating stalemate – that was until Porsche's life was made far simpler when Ferrari's challenge imploded.

ABOVE and BELOW: The magnesium-chassis 917 scored a second Le Mans victory in 1971 with Helmut Marko and Gijs van Lennep driving. PORSCHE AG

Legendary engineer Hans Mezger poses with his line of 917 creations. PORSCHE AG

The Porsche 917 set the benchmark for 1970s prototypes and is still considered one of the finest racing cars of all time. PORSCHE AG

Porsche's gamble pays off

The 312s were suffering from persistent oil leaks, which was then thrown up from the track onto windscreens by the soaking wet conditions as a period race report from *Motoring News* reads: "It may be correct to describe what happened next as a Ferrari wipe-out. Reine Wissell was bothered more than most by the oil on his screen (he'd already stopped to have it wiped) and had slowed to about 50mph in the conditions. Approaching Indianapolis corner, he was caught by Derek Bell and Clay Regazzoni and Mike Parkes, who were having a private slipstreaming battle.

"As we understand it, Bell went one way to avoid Wissell and Reggazzoni hit the Swedish driver hard in the rear. Parkes became involved too and suddenly all three cars were out of the race. Parkes' car then caught fire. On top of all that, Bell missed a gear during his excursion and over-revved his engine. So, it wasn't three, but four of the five works Ferraris out."

That became five when Jackie Ickx crashed at the Ford Chicane when his Ferrari suffered a failure of the rear brakes. His car slid into and over the sandbanks, tragically killing a marshal in the process. Ickx emerged from the blazing car unhurt, but Ferrari's challenge was done.

Porsche then had the race in the bag, with nobody to beat but itself. Yet it so nearly did, as a string of technical troubles began to hound the 917 armada.

The larger 4.9-litre engines began to struggle later in the race as the force took its toll on their gearboxes. Pedro Rodríguez was the first to go with a crankshaft failure and then the lead car of Jo Siffert headed for the pits with smoke billowing from its engine after a missed gear. The more-developed 4.5-litre engine proved more trustworthy. The wet conditions lowered the average speeds and brought the short-tailed cars into contention. The Salzburg car crewed by Hans Herrmann and Richard Attwood ran consistently to snatch the win from the Martini 917L of Gerard Larrousse and Willi Kauhsen by five clear laps.

Porsche's triumph was complete. It had finally won Le Mans at great expense and sacrifice and took with it the world sports car crown for makes. While JWA failed to finish Le Mans, it and Salzburg won every round of the 1970 championship barring Sebring to stamp Porsche's authority on the series. Porsche suddenly had the exposure it craved and with it, sales of the 911 and 917 hiked. Over 50 examples of 917 were created and sold to customers and Porsche had gone from underdog to pace-setter in a single model generation.

Porsche never ceased its development of the model. Later evolutions of the 917 featured further frontal and rear aerodynamic tweaks, chiefly the addition of vertical rear wings to the sides of the rear extension to clean up airflow from the rear arches.

Porsche dominated in 1971, with Martini Racing's magnesium chassis car of Helmut Marko and van Lennep beating Attwood and Herbert Muller's JWA entry. The two were over 30 laps clear of the fastest Ferrari in third place. Marko and van Lennep also set a distance record for Le Mans, covering 3,315 miles. That benchmark stood until 2010 when Audi's R15 TDi finally broke it by just 20 miles. Jackie Oliver also set the outright La Sarthe lap record in that race with a 3min18.30sec benchmark that will never be beaten due to the modern variation to the track.

The 917 programme was ended in Europe when the FIA banned 5.0-litre prototypes from the world championship for 1972. So Porsche had to look elsewhere. A brief foray into the American Can-Am series produced the ultimate 917 for 1973, the monstrous open-topped 917/30. This last hurrah, capable of truly terrifying speeds and power (reports claimed upwards of 1,200bhp with qualifying boost) the car swept all before it, so much so that other makes lost interest and Can-Am itself folded a year later. The 917 was then done as a factory entry, but its legend remains as strong as ever. ●

ICKX'S RECOVERY MASTERCLASS

When Porsche looked down and out during the early stages of the 1977 Le Mans 24 Hours, it made the call to install its star driver in the other car. What followed was perhaps the greatest recovery drive in the race's history.

Jacky Ickx aboard the Porsche 936 that he took to victory at Le Mans in 1977… somehow. PORSCHE AG

With six wins at the Le Mans 24 Hours, Belgian superstar Jacky Ickx is one of the most prolific drivers in the history of the great race. Sitting second in the overall all-time win tally – second only to the phenomenon that is Tom Kristensen with an otherworldly score of nine – Ickx has plenty of memories to draw from when it comes to his personal highlights. But only one really sticks out, the 1977 race, where he almost single-handedly dragged Porsche from the doldrums to the top step of the podium, albeit with a little help from the rival Alpine-Renault team.

"Of all my participations in the Le Mans 24 Hours, 1977 is the first that should be remembered because that race was all but lost," recalled Ickx. "I should never have won that year, Porsche should never have won that year, but from a lost race we got a winning opportunity and it was beautiful. There aren't many races like that in the life of a driver."

Heading into Le Mans that year, Porsche was firmly on the back foot. Its ageing 936 prototype lacked the pace of the more modern Alpine-Renaults in the field, a fact rammed home when Jean-Pierre Jabouille scorched to pole, his effort being over a second faster than he'd managed a year earlier when he also topped the timesheets. Ickx gave it everything he had, but could only manage third, almost two seconds off, as Alpine-Renaults swarmed around him within the rest of the top five.

But Le Mans isn't about outright speed, it's about reliability and consistency. The problem was Porsche didn't even have the former, although Ickx was certainly blessed with the latter.

The problems began when the sister Porsche of Jürgen Barth and Hurley Haywood returned stuttering to the pits with a faulty fuel pump after just two hours. Then, Ickx's team-mate, Henri Pescarolo, crawled his way back too, billowing smoke after just 45 laps, the cause eventually traced to a irreparably holed piston. Porsche was done. Or was it?

By the time Pescarolo had vaulted out of his stricken 936, the other car has been repaired. Yes, it had lost 30 minutes and languished down in 41st place, some 15 laps behind the runaway Alpine-Renaults, but at least it was working.

Seeing as Ickx had yet to drive, the rules allowed him to be plugged into the other car alongside Barth/Haywood. And it was then that Porsche's luck began to change.

Ickx was given free rein to drive as he liked. Damn the car and damn the result – there was nothing to lose. Better to fail trying than suffer the embarrassment of both works Porsches being out within the opening hours.

Ickx set off on what will go down in history as one of the great recovery drives. Across the course of a mammoth 11-hour stint through the night and into Sunday morning, he wrung the neck of the 936, lapping essentially at qualifying pace and even breaking François Cevert's four-year-old lap record as he tried and reel in the Alpine-Renaults.

His efforts forced the French team to up its pace and the tide began to turn when the car of Patrick Tambay/Jean-Pierre Jaussaud dropped out of third at 3am with an engine devoid of oil pressure. Then, an hour later, Jacques Laffite/Patrick Depairre's A442 dropped a cog and had to stop for an hour to have its gearbox rebuilt.

A magic marathon

By now, Ickx was second, having recovered nine of the 15 laps to the leading Alpine.

Ickx was plugged into car 4 at late notice and completed a mammoth 11-hour stint to haul it back to the front against the Alpine-Renaults. PORSCHE AG

His maximum stint time struck at 9.10am, when he was forced to hand across to Barth, but Ickx's efforts had taken their toll on the Alpines and, just minutes later, Jabouille's engine exploded in a cloud of smoke when a piston holed as he was on full throttle along the Hunaudieres. The car that had led for 17 hours was out and Alpine-Renault's hopes were in tatters.

Advantage Porsche, but things still weren't settled. With a huge 16-lap lead, Porsche reduced its pace, which proved to be a near-fatal error. Within the final hour, with Haywood at the wheel, smoke began to rise from the Porsche's tail and soon Haywood was back in the pits with Porsche's engineers scurrying to determine the issue.

The weaker fuel mixture had melted a piston, but it was still possible for the car to run. The turbos were disconnected and the piston isolated and spark plug removed. Porsche chose Barth to conduct the final run, on account of his mechanical knowledge as a dealer of Porsche race cars. With a huge ⤵

The win wasn't all about Ickx. Jürgen Barth played a vital role, managing the wounded car to the finish in the last hour. PORSCHE AG

Barth is reunited with the winning 936 for a test run at Hockenheim. PORSCHE AG

clock strapped to his steering wheel to aid the countdown to the flag, Barth limped the 936 back onto the circuit with just minutes to go to complete two final laps.

"I was terrified," said Ickx. "I couldn't watch. I went back to the motorhome and closed my eyes and crossed my fingers and I was always listening for the sound of a dying engine. I crossed my fingers so hard I got cramps in them. Nothing could be taken for granted in that last hour."

But Barth did it, crawling across the line at 4pm, 11 laps ahead of the Mirage in second place.

"It was incredible, at the finish… everyone was crying. Everyone!" recalled Ickx. "It was so unexpected this win and the emotion of it hit everybody hard, from the troubles early in the race to the troubles at the end. The Alpine-Renaults dominated, but didn't make the distance and then we nearly didn't make it. We were driving with God's good grace that day and that protected us for sure." ●

Porsche's 936 is somewhat of a forgotten Le Mans hero, going on to score a total of three victories between 1977-1981. PORSCHE AG

The heart of the beast, the turbocharged 2.1-litre engine.
PORSCHE AG

SUBSCRIBE
TO YOUR FAVOURITE MAGAZINE
AND SAVE

Classic Land Rover is an exciting monthly magazine dedicated to Series and the classic Land Rovers. Written by enthusiasts, it is the complete guide to buying, owning, running, driving, repairing, modifying and restoring pre-nineties Land Rovers and Range Rover classics.

classiclandrover.com

Porsche's new 956 locks out the front row for Le Mans 1982, signalling the start of the mighty Group C era. GETTY IMAGES

THE RISE OF THE
MONSTERS

To many, Le Mans reached its zenith during the Group C era of the 1980s. Manufacturers flooded back, bringing with them poster-boy cars that were more muscular and powerful than ever. This was the time when beasts stalked La Sarthe — and we loved it.

Ask any sports car racing fans when their favourite era of competition was and chances are the words 'Group C' will be pretty close to the top of the list of answers. Born in 1982 as a reaction to rapidly falling interest in top-flight prototype racing, what began life a simple fuel efficiency formula gradually morphed into a playground for giants.

Porsche, Jaguar, Ford, Lancia, Peugeot, Nissan, Mazda and even Mercedes-Benz (after its three-decade break) were drawn back to slug it out with cars that were the peak of technology at the time, often running monstrous engines of all shapes and varieties. The sponsorship trends that had got up a head of steam during the 1970s continued unabated into the 1980s with tobacco, alcohol, fuel and fashion companies lighting

up the grid and creating some of the most iconic liveries in the sport.

Perhaps it's the effect of those old rose-tinted spectacles, but Le Mans reached not only peak speed and power, but also peak sex appeal during the Group C era.

The story began in 1980. Local legend Jean Rondeau began the decade by making his own piece of history, becoming the first and so far only driver ever to win the Le Mans 24 Hours

Key Moments

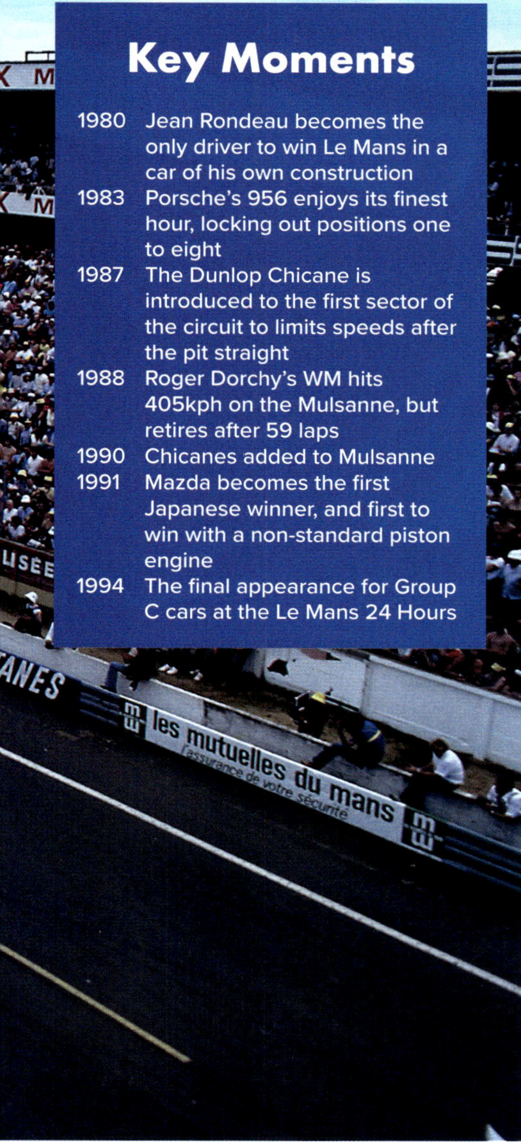

Key Moments

1980   Jean Rondeau becomes the only driver to win Le Mans in a car of his own construction

1983   Porsche's 956 enjoys its finest hour, locking out positions one to eight

1987   The Dunlop Chicane is introduced to the first sector of the circuit to limits speeds after the pit straight

1988   Roger Dorchy's WM hits 405kph on the Mulsanne, but retires after 59 laps

1990   Chicanes added to Mulsanne

1991   Mazda becomes the first Japanese winner, and first to win with a non-standard piston engine

1994   The final appearance for Group C cars at the Le Mans 24 Hours

Porsche's 956 set the early pace for Group C straight away, quickly becoming the car to beat. PORSCHE AG

the challenge of going as fast and as far as they could on 600 litres of fuel per race.

This challenge proved a real leveller. During previous years, many teams had gained advantages by simply upsizing engines or increasing turbo boost pressures, leading to huge development costs. Do that in Group C and you'd be rapid, but you'd never finish. It was the ultimate balancing act and suddenly all types of engines could race in relative parity, be they turbocharged, naturally aspirated, V12, V8 or even rotary.

Porsche, Ford and Lancia were the first to commit to building cars, but it would be the Germans who got the flying start, even if it wasn't immediately obvious. The legendary

driving a car of his own construction. As you will read later, it was the culmination of a near-ruinous personal obsession for Rondeau. But, in truth, the victory was taken during a year when the works teams firmly switched off from Le Mans. Unswayed by the current Group 5 (for open-topped prototypes) and Group 6 (for closed ones) rules, Rondeau outlasted a thin and largely privateer field.

Porsche's works team returned for 1981 with the now positively ancient 936. It had evolved considerably since its debut in 1976, but this was still a five-year-old design at heart. Jacky Ickx and Derek Bell cruised to the win before the entire endurance racing landscape would change.

Enter Group C, enter Porsche

In an attempt to reinvigorate both Le Mans and the World Endurance Championship, the FIA came up with a plan to build on the current GTP rules for closed-cockpit prototypes. Within a set of size and weight parameters, manufacturers could build whatever sort of chassis they liked and put whatever engine they fancied at the heart of it. The sole stipulation was that they would be allowed a maximum fuel capacity of 100kg and would be made to make five refuelling stops across the course of a 1,000km race. Effectively, teams were set

The Winners

1980
Rondeau M379
Jean Rondeau/Jean-Pierre Jaussaud, 4308km

1981
Porsche 936
Jacky Ickx/Derek Bell, 4825km

1982
Porsche 956
Jacky Ickx/Derek Bell, 4899km

1983
Porsche 956
Vern Schuppan/Hurley Haywood/Al Holbert, 5048km

1984
Porsche 956B
Henri Pescarolo/Klaus Ludwig, 4900km

1985
Porsche 956B
Klaus Ludwig/Paolo Barilla/'John Winter', 5089km

1986
Porsche 962C
Derek Bell/Hans Joachim Stuck/Al Holbert, 4973km

1987
Porsche 962C
Derek Bell/Hans Joachim Stuck/Al Holbert, 4792km

1988
Jaguar XJR-9LM
Jan Lammers/Johnny Dumfries/Andy Wallace, 5333km

1989
Sauber C9
Jochen Mass/Manuel Reuter/Stanley Dickens, 5262km

1990
Jaguar XJR-12
John Nielsen/Price Cobb/Martin Brundle, 4882km

1991
Mazda 787B
Volker Weidler/Johnny Herbert/Bertrand Gachot, 4923km

1992
Peugeot 905 Evo 1B
Derek Warwick/Yannick Dalmas/Mark Blundell, 4787km

1993
Peugeot 905 Evo 1B
Eric Hélary/Christophe Bouchut/Geoff Brabham, 5100km

1994
Dauer 962 Le Mans
Yannick Dalmas/Hurley Haywood/Mauro Baldi, 4686km

Mercedes-Benz returned with its fearsome Sauber C9s and secured a one-two finish in 1989. MERCEDES-BENZ

That would be the turning point and 962s would then go on to dominate for the next two years. No other brand got a look-in as Porsche extended its winning streak to seven years (counting the 936 of 1981).

But new challengers were on the way and soon Porsche would have a true fight on its hands. American Bob Tullius was a big fan of two things: Jaguar and Le Mans. Having campaigned self-built specials in the US under his Group 44 banner, he garnered some support from British Leyland's US importer.

It was through this link that Tullius convinced Jaguar to help fund a new prototype for IMSA, the XJR-5, in 1982. By 1984, Jaguar was back at Le Mans as Tullius brought two cars to take on the Porsches. One did briefly lead during the opening round of pit stops, but then a combination of punctures and gearbox issues put paid to them. There would be a repeat attempt in 1985, when the car won the GTP class, though it ultimately finished 13th overall.

956 initially didn't look all that legendary, largely thanks to a hotch-potch entry for its first race at Silverstone leading to different cars running to different rule sets.

Based around an aluminium monocoque, with Kevlar bodywork and a 2.5-litre engine from the 936 plonked inside it with a few turbos bolted on, the 956 had all the ingredients to shine. It did exactly that when Ickx put the car on pole at Silverstone, 1.5 seconds clear of the best of the older Lancias.

During the race, however, the 956s had to conserve fuel to abide by the five stops rule, whereas the old Group 6 Lancias didn't. Cue a farce as the Porsches trundled round 10 seconds a lap off the pace while the Lancias ran away with it. But, come Le Mans, when the fuel rules were more preferable, there would be no answer to what would become one of the most dominant sportscars of all-time.

Bell and Ickx would lead a podium whitewash in 1982 as the three works 956s demolished the field. The marginally better fuel efficiency of the Rondeaus and Fords made it a bit of a race early on, but soon the 956's sheer rampant pace put the result beyond doubt. That would be the start of a quartet of wins at La Sarthe as Porsche tightened its stranglehold on Le Mans. By selling numerous cars to customers, 956s soon became by far the most populous model on the grid, so even if the factory didn't win, chances were an affiliate team would. In fact, between 1982 and 1985, only one car that wasn't a 956 would finish on the outright podium, and even that was another Porsche.

Porsche vs IMSA

IMSA was getting tired of Porsche dominating across the pond so, in an effort to out-regulate the 956, the Americans altered the safety rules, demanding a driver's feet must be behind the front axle line in all cars. Porsche put its drivers up front as far as possible to even weight – some drivers even insisted their feet were the main frontal crash structure in the old 917 – so it looked like the 956 was out.

But IMSA hadn't reckoned with the level of German ingenuity at play and soon the 956 became the 962, essentially a carry-over car but with the wheelbase lengthened to move the pedal box back to the legal zone

behind the front wheels. The 962 made its debut at Le Mans in 1984, leading before its gearbox gave out, and then another car finished third in 1985 to (sort of) break the 956 hegemony.

Jaguar returns… properly

Tullius had expected to continue the programme, but Jaguar's top brass had other ideas. In September that year the firm signed a contract with Tom Walkinshaw Racing to create

The Group C rules were successful in drawing manufacturers back to sports car racing. Here Mercedes, Jaguar, Nissan, Porsche and Toyota go toe-to-toe at Silverstone in 1990. GETTY IMAGES

What started out as a fuel efficiency formula soon spiralled into one of the greatest wars between manufacturers Le Mans has ever witnessed. MERCEDES-BENZ

Derek Bell is lofted high with the champagne after victory in 1987. This was the last of his five Le Mans wins, making him one of the all-time most successful drivers. GETTY IMAGES

Bob Tullius' Group 44 team brought Jaguar back to Le Mans, until the factory and TWR properly took over. GETTY IMAGES

the XJR-6, Jaguar's first full-works Le Mans entry since the 1950s, much to Tullius' chagrin. But the XJR-6's debut in 1986 didn't go well. While bestowed with great top speed on the Mulsanne, all three of its cars retired, beset by gearbox, driveshaft and fuelling issues (one simply ran out!).

The new XJR-8 for 1987 enjoyed more success, taking Jaguar to fifth at Le Mans, even if a catastrophic tyre failure sent driver Win Percy into the air along the Mulsanne at north of 220mph. Fortunately, the car's carbon/Kevlar monocoque proved enough to protect him from serious injury.

Then the game-changing XJR-9 came on stream for 1988. Designed by Tony Southgate as an evolution of the XJR-8, the 9 featured a raft of upgrades over its predecessor and represented Jaguar's best chance of toppling Porsche, which had pulled its works team out of the World Sportscar Championship but would return for Le Mans. However, it was Jaguar that had the momentum and the added bonus of data acquired from running at all WSC rounds.

The XJR-9 was arguably the finest example of the TWR Jaguars. It was the culmination of a constant development cycle and now based on proven and known technology. It also

benefited from some key changes to the Group C rules. A reduction in wheel size from 19in to 17in inadvertently cured one of the XJR's biggest issues. It lowered the car's rear axle, meaning there was no longer a requirement to run tilted driveshafts, and the team was able to refit the rear wheel covers, or 'spats', to boost aerodynamic efficiency.

The XJR-9 also featured a remodelled and strengthened March gearbox offering improved wishbone mounting points and remodelled rear suspension. TWR had started to experiment with some ingenious engineering concepts, such as the inclusion of a fuel return pipe, which ran alongside the inlet manifold to effectively chill the fuel upon delivery. This meant the XJR-9 could shed the weight of a dedicated fuel cooler.

Three-way fight – at first

Le Mans 1988 had been shaping up to be a three-way fight between Porsche, Jaguar and the returning Mercedes-Benz team, now in partnership with Sauber. The potent Mercedes-powered C9 was entered by the works outfit for the first time in 1988, but didn't actually start the event as the cars were pulled following tyre failures in practice, put down to the newly-resurfaced Mulsanne Straight and the car's downforce combining to generate more friction and heat than its Michelin tyres could handle.

That set up a Porsche vs Jaguar epic that would feature an incredible tale of quick thinking from Dutchman Jan Lammers. Porsches grabbed pole on increased boost, a full six seconds faster than the best of the Jaguars, but come the race their engines had to be tuned back down to go the distance, whereas the hulking 7.0-litre Jaguar V12s could breathe as normal. The Jaguars blew past the 962s on the second lap and never looked back. However, it was still far from an easy run.

When the #3 Jag trundled into the pits to retire with a terminal gearbox issue after 129 laps, Lammers overheard Brazilian driver ➲

Jaguar's breakthrough in 1988 when its XJR-9LM finally broke Porsche's stranglehold, cheered on by thousands of British fans. GETTY IMAGES

Jaguar's victory was assured by some quick-thinking by Dutchman Jan Lammers. GETTY IMAGES

Raul Boesel describing the feeling that pre-empted the problem.

"Raul said he went from second to third and it jumped out of gear and then he went from third to fourth and it jumped again and then failed completely," Lammers recalled. "I went in for the last few hours in the lead and I'm just into my stint when I go from second to third and it jumps out of gear and I just had those words ringing in my head. It was impossible that we would lose this race, so I went from third to fourth and it engaged the gear, so at that moment I said I was never touching that gear-lever again! I had to be smooth to try and not stress anything, no full throttle and just trundle the car around. But we had a pit stop to do, but I knew I could slip the clutch and get the car going again in fourth gear. The mechanics knew there was a problem, but nobody wanted to say anything and curse it."

Lammers somehow drove for over an hour using only fourth gear, doing just enough to secure victory for himself, Johnny Dumfries and Andy Wallace ahead of the rapidly gaining Porsche of Derek Bell/Hans-Joachim Stuck/ Klaus Ludwig, which had lost time when it ran dry of fuel earlier in the race.

But how close had Jaguar come to disaster? "When they took the gearbox apart after the race the secondary shaft was split in the middle," said Lammers. "One more change and it would all have fallen apart."

Speeds and skulduggery

That 1988 race will also go down in history as one that changed the Circuit de la Sarthe forever. The small Welter Racing team had been a regular at Le Mans, but it wasn't particularly concerned with the race itself, more to push the boundaries of what could be achieved on the Mulsanne. Run by what was essentially a group of factory Peugeot engineers on a jolly, the team formed a programme known as 'The 400 Club', which would put performance above reliability in order to try and be the first to achieve 400kph at Le Mans.

Parisian garage owner Roger Dorchy would achieve it, wringing the neck of the 2.8-litre turbocharged WM P88 during Saturday evening to be officially recorded at 405kph (251mph) through the speed trap. In fact, WM was convinced it had gone even quicker, but it was decided that 405kph would be declared in deference to the Peugeot engine that was pushing out 900bhp in the back. The brand's 405 saloon launched that year.

Team Sauber-Mercedes would also clock 400kph the following year when its C9 for Jochen Mass/Manuel Reiter/Stanley Dickens came good to score a one-two for the Silver Arrows, Mercedes' first victory at Le Mans since 1952. But this game of chance would soon be over, thanks to political wrangling that would neuter the Mulsanne for good from 1990.

In 1987 Bernie Ecclestone was installed as the FIA's vice-president of promotional affairs, putting him in charge of the commercial rights for all FIA-sanctioned series, of which the World Sports-Prototype Championship was one. But Le Mans had its own broadcast deals and handing across its commercial rights in the same way Formula 1 had made little sense.

Political wrangling

So, when the Circuit de la Sarthe's track licence came up for renewal in 1989, the commercial rights deals became a political bargaining tool. The straight could stay as it was if a deal could be struck. One wasn't, so then-FIA President Jean-Marie Balestre issued a new rule limiting the length of any single straight to 1.2-miles in the name of safety.

Two chicanes were installed along the Mulsanne and have been there ever since. It acted to set Dorchy's record in stone, with only Mark Blundell getting close when he registered 366kph (226.9mph) in the dangerously over-boosting Nissan R90C during qualifying in

The Group C rules also brought big crowds and teams from across the world.

Porsche used some cunning engineering to turn the 956 into the 962, moving the driver further back in the chassis to satisfy IMSA rules. PORSCHE AG

1990. It would be the last lap that particular engine ever did.

That 1990 race brought a second victory for Jaguar, but only after some unscrupulous driver shuffling. Martin Brundle was Walkinshaw's golden boy so, when his XJR-12 developed a water leak while leading and lost a heap of time in the pits, team boss Tom Walkinshaw came up with a plan. Ordering Brundle to rest over the night, but not leave the track, Walkinshaw kept John Nielsen and Price Cobb alternating in the #3 car, while official third driver Eliseo Salazar waited patiently for his turn at the wheel. But it would never arrive.

The rules said each car may only have three drivers, so by keeping Salazar hanging around, Walkinshaw could plug Brundle straight into the sister car in the morning. The effect was shattering for Salazar, who quit sports car racing there and then. Despite the winning car that year still bearing his name and the Chilean flag, he didn't hang around to see it take the finish.

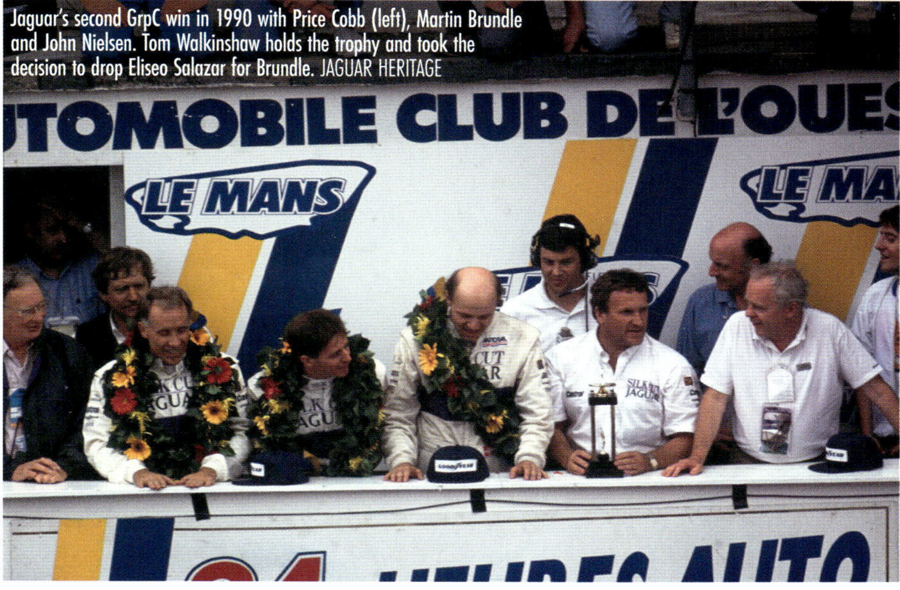

Jaguar's second GrpC win in 1990 with Price Cobb (left), Martin Brundle and John Nielsen. Tom Walkinshaw holds the trophy and took the decision to drop Eliseo Salazar for Brundle. JAGUAR HERITAGE

The fall of a legend

Group C continued unabated until the rule-makers became a victim of their own success. By 1989, sports car racing was almost as popular as F1, so there seemed an obvious opportunity to exchange technology, and perhaps manufacturers, between the two.

The rules were changed to strongly suggest that teams switched to running 3.5-litre engines similar to those used in F1 at the time. Any cars that didn't, such as the Jaguars and Porsches, would be laden with ballast to restrict their performance and drop down a class. Both Mazda and Peugeot were the chief beneficiaries of this. Firstly, Mazda somehow managed to persuade the rule-makers that its rotary 787B fell outside the ballast rules before springing a shock win in 1991 (explored later) and then Peugeot beat thin or limited opposition with its 3.5-litre 905 Evo in 1992/93.

Seen as a thinly-veiled attempt to poach manufacturers from sports car racing, the change in engine rules wasn't popular. Plus, in a perhaps non-shocking twist, sourcing F1-spec engines proved rather costly. Budgets spiralled and interest waned so badly that grids rapidly fell away, leading the 1993 world championship to be scrapped before it even started.

Group C had its final hurrah at Le Mans in 1994 and it was perhaps fitting that a retro-grade classic would win, in the form of Dauer's 962 Le Mans, essentially a Porsche 962 that had been converted to street legality and then entered as a GT1 car.

Some 12 years after the first appearance of the 956, Porsche's design had outlived the category that gave it life and was still winning, at least for one final time before being outlawed entirely. That's staying power. ●

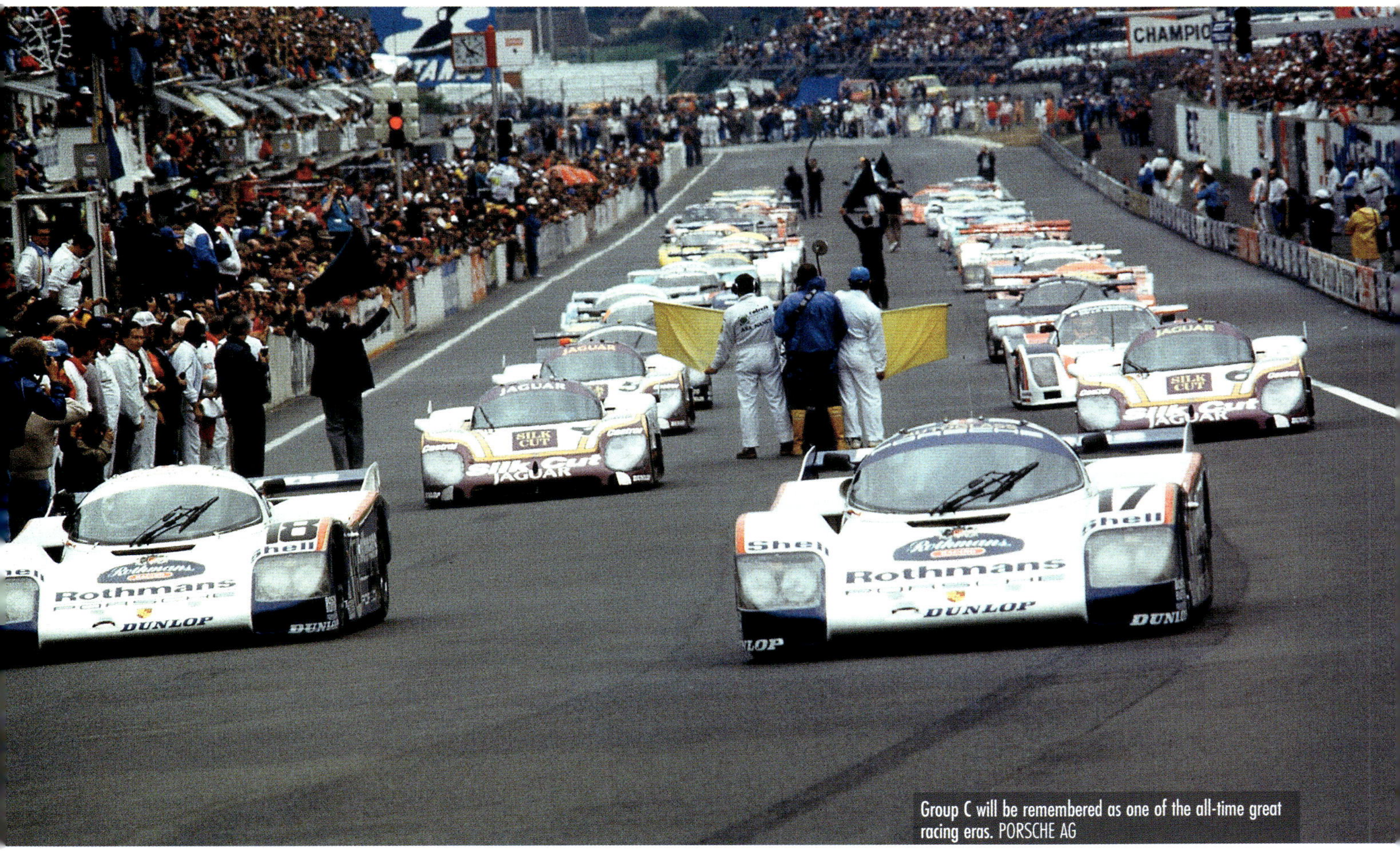

Group C will be remembered as one of the all-time great racing eras. PORSCHE AG

THE ULTIMATE
HOMEGROWN HERO

Jean Rondeau stands alone as the only driver ever to win the Le Mans 24 Hours in a car of his own making. It would be the culmination of a lifelong ambition and an almost ruinous five-year campaign. This is his story.

The Sarthe locals knew the drill pretty well. If you heard that distinctive Cosworth roar and that unfamiliar shape loomed in your mirrors, indicate and pull over. Jean Rondeau was coming through.

Sounds the stuff of science fiction, but it was reality for the town of Le Mans during the late 1970s when one man, driven relentlessly forward by a desire to make history in his own back yard, pushed boundaries in every way possible. If that meant taking his latest racing prototype for a spin on the nearby RN138 'Ligne Droite des Hunaudières', more commonly known to us as the Mulsanne Straight, then so be it. Police would stand and watch. They knew it was just Jean Rondeau doing Jean Rondeau things.

Although the Rondeau story is brief, the marque and the man shone brightly when, in 1980, he and team-mate Jean-Pierre Jaussaud achieved what many had believed impossible, winning the Le Mans 24 Hours in a car bearing the name Rondeau and manufactured a short walk from the track. Nobody has equalled Rondeau's feat since – and in all likelihood never will, amid a modern racing world awash with manufacturer teams running multi-million-pound precision racing instruments. Rondeau's win owed something to luck, but it was more than deserved after years of toil and living almost hand-to-mouth, moving from one shaky deal to the next to stay afloat.

Back where it all began. After several attempts in poor machinery, Rondeau constructed the first Inaltéra for 1976. This is Henri Pescarolo driving a restored one. GETTY IMAGES

Jean Rondeau is carried by the public following his historic victory at Le Mans in 1980, during which he became the only driver ever to win in a car bearing his own name. GETTY IMAGES

l'Ouest called the Alpine Cup, which would aim to find and support undiscovered racing talent, the ultimate prize being a seat in an Alpine A210 for Le Mans. Rondeau finished second in the first stage of selection but was then let go and the chance eventually fell to Christian Ethuin and Bob Wollek.

Talent spotted

Regardless, Rondeau had been spotted by another local, François Migault, the winner of the previous year's contest. And the pair's careers would be intertwined from there.

Realising it would take cash rather than good fortune to make it to Le Mans, Rondeau took a job in an interior design shop, where he eventually became the sales manager and earned enough to compete in a few hillclimb events to sharpen his skills before his big chance came along for 1972.

Migault was already by then an established sportscar driver and had been sharing a Chevron B21 with British driver Brian Robinson in the World Sportscar Championship. But, when notable team owner Charles Pozzi came calling with a chance to contest Le Mans aboard his Ferrari 365, Migault suggested that Rondeau slot in alongside Robinson. His Le Mans debut was cut short when the Chevron's engine gave up after 10 hours, but he'd got a taste of it now and wanted more.

For 1973, he bought a seat in an amateur effort running a Porsche 908 but failed to qualify. The following year they returned, managed to qualify and went on to finish 19th – the penultimate car left running – but at least Rondeau could now claim to have actually finished the Le Mans 24 Hours. The 1975 race brought no improvement as Rondeau drove the hopelessly outclassed Mazda RX3, which qualified 50th and gave up 13 hours in.

This simply wasn't good enough, so Rondeau vowed to do things his own way from then on.

The early 1970s were a boom time for the French at Le Mans. Matra had taken ➙

Yet, just five years on from that historic Le Mans triumph, Rondeau would be dead. He led a gambler's life but had rolled the dice one too many times when he attempted to race a train across a level crossing. It was an ending as bizarre as his story.

Born and raised in Le Mans, Rondeau lived virtually every day of his life within a stone's throw of the Circuit de la Sarthe and first discovered the 24 Hours when he was just three, taken as a spectator by his father. As soon as he could, he told his parents he would grow up to be a racing driver and the Le Mans 24 Hours would be his aim.

Rondeau's competitive spirit was clear from an early age. As a child he took part in scooter races around the city centre, constantly striving to gain an advantage over the rest by modifying his scooters with lighter wheels and upgraded brakes. As a student, he promised his parents he would do well at school, but only if they pledged to take him to Le Mans, scrutineering each year so he could immerse himself alongside the teams and cars, listening to every detail.

In 1968, aged 22, he took part in a talent search organised by the Automobile Club de

Drivers Bernard Darnich (left) and Rondeau pose with the Rondeau M378 ahead of the 1978 Le Mans. GETTY IMAGES

A local to Le Mans, Rondeau was born and raised within a stone's throw of the circuit, so made it his mission to conquer the great race. GETTY IMAGES

virtually build a car in the race's backyard. He asked if I could help with testing and development and then said: 'Do you think you could help us with sponsorship too?'"

Elford suggested he was no good at that sort of thing, but inadvertently he was. Elford had a connection with Charles James, the new boss of the Inaltéra wallpaper company, who was keen to back a racing project. With his own background in interior design sales, it proved a perfect match to back Rondeau, so a deal was struck and work began.

At the time Le Mans rules were graduating toward new Grand Touring Prototype, or GTP, rules, allowing brands to create closed-in racing cars to set dimensions with off-the-shelf engines from recognised brands, which would eventually be a forerunner to Group C.

Rondeau fancied this method and foresaw the growth of the GTP rules so was an early adopter. He brought together a team of friends and family (including the famous Beaumesnil family and former Porsche and Matra aerodynamicist Robert Choulet) and formed ATAC (short for Association pour la Vulgarisation & le Promotion des Techniques de Courses Automobiles, the association for the popularisation and promotion of motor racing techniques) to design the car.

Key to Rondeau's success was a crack squad of some of the very best French drivers. Henri Pescarolo joined after losing out on a Ligier F1 drive. GETTY IMAGES

the first homegrown win for 22 years in 1972 to kick-start a hat-trick of successes, but withdrew after 1974, leaving Ligier as the sole competitor. French industrialists were keen to keep the run going and see more teams sporting the Tricolore, so sponsorship opportunities were out there. It was just a matter of putting together the right connections and people.

Enter, Vic Elford, who told *Motor Sport*: "I got a call from Rondeau, who I didn't know at the time. I think he just knew I lived in France and had a reputation for being a good test driver. He told me about this project – to

Originally a team made up almost exclusively of family and friends, the Rondeau organisation quickly grew. Here the squad services the 1979 M379 as Jean watches on. GETTY IMAGES

Terrible conditions greeted fans and media during the 1980 race, but they would witness a bit of history. GETTY IMAGES

Testing begins

Using a 1:5-scale model tested at the Eiffel wind tunnel in Paris, the numbers were encouraging and just a few months later, the first Inaltéra GTP was born and with distinct Formula 1 influence. Not only was it powered by the same 3.0-litre V8 Ford Cosworth DFV that was flying high in F1, but Rondeau scooped up both Jean-Pierre Beltoise and Henri Pescarolo to drive when Ligier unceremoniously dumped both from its testing team on the eve of its F1 entry.

Armed with two of the best French drivers around and a car that was ferociously fast on the straights, the Inaltéra made people sit up and take notice. There were teething problems, but Beltoise and Pescarolo finished eighth with Rondeau/Jaussaud/Christine Beckers 21st. Both cars took the finish first time out and the foundations had been laid. The following year Rondeau and Jean Ragnotti finished fourth. Everything seemed to be on the up until a management shuffle at Inaltéra pulled the proverbial rug. The funding was gone, the cars sold and ATAC liquidated. Rondeau's dreams were in tatters, but he wasn't about to quit.

Rondeau had a key ally in the form of Marjorie Brosse, the wife of the Mayor of Le Mans and a woman with far-reaching political connections. And she would prove his saviour, rustling up enough backing for Rondeau to start a new car design and providing workshops on the nearby Montehard industrial estate.

After toying with the idea of a six-wheeler similar to the Tyrrel P34 F1 machine, the Rondeau M378 (the M standing for Marjorie) was constructed for 1978 out of the original Inaltéra plans and a single car appeared at Le Mans. Rondeau and team-mate Bernard Darniche finished ninth, winning the GTP class for the third consecutive year.

A year later and Marjorie had been at it again, this time finding backing significant enough to move the team to a new base in Champagne and give the cars a total aerodynamic overhaul. With vastly improved wind tunnel figures and better-tuned Cosworths, the M379 proved 26 seconds a lap faster in qualifying than its predecessor. Ragnotti and Darniche finished fifth at Le Mans, with Pescarolo/Beltoise 10th. And then the coffers ran dry again.

The solution this time was to hire out a third car, with the paying customers essentially part-funding the main crews. And Rondeau found customers in the form of the Martin brothers, Jean-Michel and Phillippe, who were adept at touring car racing, but sportscars would be another matter entirely. The Belgian pair had been competing with Ford Capris regularly at the 24 Hours of Spa, with British ace Gordon Spice acting as team-mate, coach and crew chief in the Belgo-backed saloons.

Spice recalled: "When the Martins told me they'd hired this Rondeau to do Le Mans, I thought they were mad! Capris were one thing, but this was a 200mph prototype and they had no clue. I agreed to share with them ➲

Rondeau and Jaussaud's M379B would go on to take a narrow victory after an eventful 24 hours. GETTY IMAGES

The local lad done good: crossing the line to make history in 1980. GETTY IMAGES

on the condition they did absolutely everything I said and never deviated from the plan."

Adding Spice to the mix

Spice, who would become the only British driver ever to race for the Rondeau team, remembers arriving to a difficult environment with the highly nationalistic French team at first, but earning his place through a rather unusual initiation.

"I brought my team manager Keith Greene with me to look after our car and when we first arrived we were soundly ignored," said Spice. "I remember on the first night of practice it was foul, absolutely pouring down, and nobody batted an eyelid our way as we were just the rental drivers. I said to Keith 'set the car up for the wet, KG, I'm going to have a crack…' and of course that meant the other cars had to go out too as they didn't want to sit and watch this Englishman go brave it. I did a storming lap, a real knife-edge job with the car all over the place, but about 15 seconds faster than anyone.

"After that, we went back to the big farmhouse Rondeau had at Mierre and the other drivers said to me 'How did you do that time?' so I responded quite nonchalantly: 'That was just a normal lap for me… Keith made the car good and I just drove it'. I said to them 'trouble with you lads is you're so image conscious… drinking loads of water and going for runs… so you probably don't sleep well at night. Try a few rums instead, that'll sort you out!' By the Friday we'd run out of my rum and I had to send my chauffeur off to Paris to go buy another crate of Captain Morgan! That's what got Keith and myself integrated and we kept getting invited back for the next three years.

"I got on well with Jean. During the 1980 race he came up to me and said: 'Gordon, *Voulez Vous Faire un double*' and I misunderstood him and said: 'No Jean, the problem with 24-hour races

Jaussaud waves to the crowd with Rondeau behind. It would be Jean-Pierre's second and final Le Mans win following his success with Alpine-Renault in 1978. GETTY IMAGES

is that you can't have a drink when racing...' and then my wife turned to me and said 'don't be daft, he asked if you wanted to do a double stint!'. I thought he was offering me a double rum and Coke! He would only speak English to you if he really had to. Otherwise, it was your job to fit in. It's amazing how fast you can learn the language if you're forced into it."

That year's Le Mans would be something of an outlier in that the big works teams like Porsche and Alpine-Renault dropped out of the top Group 6 class, instead focusing on more production-spec GT models. That left the door wide open for a privateer to score – and Rondeau walked right through it. Just.

With the biggest opposition coming from a modified Porsche 908 entered by Reinhold Joest and Jacky Ickx, the race itself became a straight fight between both the two cars and the elements.

After struggling with ignition issues in qualifying, Rondeau and Jaussaud would start back in 11th, with Pescarolo/Ragnotti in third. The race started in persistent rain and the Rondeau team's challenge hit its first stumbling block when Pescarolo ground to a halt on the Mulsanne with a blown head gasket just before midnight on Saturday.

Ickx assumed the lead and built a lap's advantage over the Jaussaud/Rondeau car, which had worked its way up the order thanks to Jaussaud's pace. Cue a tight game of cat-and-mouse between the two as they exchanged the lead during pit stops. Then Jaussaud had to stop for a brake change on Sunday morning, seemingly handing the advantage to the Joest Porsche, but just an hour later the Porsche was in the pits after losing fifth gear.

The car lost 25 minutes stationary, handing Jaussaud and Rondeau back the lead. But there would be another twist when the rain that had abated for much of the morning suddenly ➲

Scenes on the podium as the jubilant pair celebrate. GETTY IMAGES

Gordon Spice joined the Rondeau team as part of the deal for the Martin brothers to rent this car for 1980. They would go on to score a podium and a class win, despite being more used to Ford Capris. GETTY IMAGES

returned, drenching the track. Rondeau got caught out on some standing water at the Dunlop Curve, sliding off and swiping the barrier. He recovered just in time to see the Joest-driven Porsche do the same thing.

Both teams continued and pitted as one on the same lap in the final 40 minutes, with Jaussaud taking over from Rondeau and Ickx back in the Porsche. Moments later, the heavens opened again. Ickx dived back into the pits to fit wet tyres, hoping the rain would last and he could overwhelm the Rondeau, which Jaussaud had opted to keep out on its slicks.

Total exhaustion

"Jean had been in the gravel once that morning already and his lap times were getting slower and slower," Jaussaud recalled to *DailySportsCar*. "Ickx was gaining fast, so we had to pit and I took over. I discovered after the race that Jean was totally exhausted and dehydrated. He was having dialysis while I was finishing the race."

The rain did cease and there would be no way back for Ickx as Jaussaud nursed the Rondeau home to record an incredible victory. Spice and the Martin brothers would not only win the GTP class in their Rondeau but also complete the overall podium in what turned out to be the all-time high for the Rondeau team.

During our interview, shortly before his death in 2021, Spice recalled the character of Rondeau: "Jean was a wild man, first and foremost, but also a bit of a mixture. He had this absolute determination to do exactly what he wanted to do and nothing else, you could call

it selfish single-mindedness. He had a whole area to play with that just so happened to be Le Mans. If he built a new prototype, or changed some suspension and wanted to test the car he'd just drive it out of the workshop and onto the roads to do it. Nobody ever said a thing to him. The police wouldn't even dare try and stop him.

"He was a gentleman, but he certainly had an arrogance. I always saw him as a great leader of men. He had a way of keeping people engaged despite bad times. Staff sometimes wouldn't get paid for weeks on end because he'd run out of money doing deals here and there, but they always kept coming into work because they trusted he would get the deals done and they would be paid."

Porsche would return in force the following year, with Ickx/Derek Bell beating the twin Rondeaus, Jean-Louis Schlesser/Philippe Streiff leading home Spice/Migault in second and third places.

The 1982 season would be the deal-breaker for the Rondeau team. After a disastrous Le Mans when all the works cars dropped out with engine trouble (traced to a faulty batch of rubber on the pick-ups for the ignition) Rondeau stayed in contention for the World Championship for Makes and should have won it but for a regulation loophole.

Porsche trailed Rondeau in the running total but spotted that a privateer 911 had scored some points at the Nürburgring and suggested they should be added to its tally. The FIA agreed and Porsche was champion, much to Rondeau's disgust. That was the start of the end, as Rondeau's sponsor withdrew amid the fallout.

Ford France financed one final effort with the turbocharged M482C in 1983, but the car proved too draggy and its 4.0-litre Cosworth DFL too unreliable. With no answer to Porsche's steamroller, Rondeau finally went belly up. The marque would deliver a few Formula Fords and Jean Rondeau would return to Le Mans as a driver, finishing a surprise second alongside American John Paul Jr in a customer Porsche 956 in 1984 and then 17th in a WM Peugeot in 1984.

For 1986, Rondeau had inked a deal to join the newly-founded Venturi effort, but he would never get there.

On December 27, 1984, Rondeau attempted to run a level crossing in Champagne, sparking disaster. As he waited in traffic aboard his Porsche 944, the crossing was briefly raised to allow an on-call police car to cross. As above the law as he may have felt, Rondeau attempted to follow it through, only to be met by the Paris-to-Quimper express train halfway. And with that this local Le Mans legend met his end, aged just 39. ●

How Rondeau should be remembered, on top of the world at home. He would be killed at a level crossing just five years after this moment. GETTY IMAGES

Later efforts wouldn't prove as successful as the big factory teams returned and Porsche's domination began. This is the 1982 car for Rondeau/Ragnotti/Pescarolo. Its engine let go after 13hrs. Two years later and the works team was gone for good, but Rondeaus would race on at Le Mans until 1988. GETTY IMAGES

GROUP C, UP CLOSE AND PERSONAL

For many, no era of the Le Mans 24 Hours packs quite the same punch as Group C. Lasting a little over a decade from 1982 until 1993, it treated La Sarthe to some of the most mind-boggling cars it had ever known. John Watson raced two of the very best. By Jim Weeks

Watson in his pomp, circa 1974. This was taken during his first full Formula 1 season aboard a Goldie Hexagon Racing Brabham. GETTY IMAGES

Having fought for the 1982 Formula 1 World Championship with McLaren, John Watson found himself at a crossroads in 1984. He'd departed the Ron Dennis-led team and, while there was an offer on the table from another grand prix outfit, he wasn't convinced. So, after a decade in Formula 1 – which included that emphatic victory in the 1983 United States West Grand Prix at Long Beach, in which he rose from 22nd on the grid to win for McLaren, still standing as the record for the lowest starting place to ever win a world championship grand prix – Watson decamped to sportscars. Within a few years, he'd raced some of the most iconic pieces of machinery in Le Mans history, including the all-conquering Porsche 956, 962 and Jaguar's XJR-9.

"My career in Formula 1 was ended by the team, not by me," he explained. "I was asked to drive for someone else in 1984, but the

Alongside his grand prix commitments, Watson began to cut his teeth in sportscars in the mid 1970s. Here he is in action at Nürburgring in a Chevron B26, shared with Peter Gethin. GETTY IMAGES

Watson's Le Mans debut came back in 1973, sharing a Mirage M6 Ford with Mike Hailwood and Vern Schuppan (number 9, rear, right). Sadly the car would be no match for the Ferraris and Matras up front. It would be 11 years before he would return again. GETTY IMAGES

manner in which it came about just didn't appeal, so I turned it down. At the same time the association that had been generated with the TAG Porsche engine (used by McLaren in 1983) provided a direct link to the Rothmans Porsche Group C team.

"I was given a test at the beginning of '84 down at Paul Ricard and I was very impressed. It didn't have the handling of an F1 car but it used ground-effect aerodynamics, the 2.65-litre turbocharged motor was bloody quick and the mid-range torque was particularly good. Eventually I got to take part in the Spa 1,000 Kilometres in September, then the Fuji 1,000 Kilometres with Stefan Bellof."

Watson and Bellof won in Japan, helping the gifted young German to be crowned World Endurance Champion for 1984. Bellof's life was cut short less than a year later in a crash at Spa, extinguishing what most believe would have gone on to be a glittering career. "Bellof was a real talent, especially in that 956," said Watson. "He might even have gone on to become an F1 world champion... he was that good. But there we are."

Watson, meanwhile, continued to build upon his relationship with Porsche. "In 1985 I was invited to join the third car at Le Mans with Vern Schuppan and Al Holbert," he said. "What Porsche had achieved with the aero balance of the 956 was really special. I'd go as far as

Before joining TWR's programme, Watson raced for the Jaguar-blessed American Group 44 team. GETTY IMAGES

Watson believes that Porsche's 962 (and before that its 956) was so successful because it was simply easy to drive in all conditions. GETTY IMAGES

to say it was the best Le Mans car I ever drove, simply because it did what it was designed to do – it was quick in a straight line but retained its balance. It was really nice to drive and I think at one point we led the race."

Mechanical luck strikes

"Unfortunately, on Sunday morning I was heading down the Mulsanne when suddenly I could hear what sounded like a cement mixer behind my head. I drove back to the pits slowly and explained that there was a problem with the motor. They took the engine cover off and that was it, we were out of the race. It turned out the engine had thrown a con rod which had gone through the block, though the thing still got me back to the pits! 1985 was the year when everyone was trying to get good fuel economy. One of the things we did was to run the engine below the normal RPM, so instead of running it to 8,000 we were at 6,500rpm and short-shifting

A moment of history at Long Beach in 1983. Watson's Le Mans luck may not have come in, but his win from 22nd is still a grand prix racing record. GETTY IMAGES

From the dominant force, Watson switched to the new pretender. Jaguar enjoyed legendary status at Le Mans thanks to its haul of five wins between 1951 and 1957, while Watson had made a one-off appearance for the British marque in 1984. Jaguar launched a serious comeback in 1986 under the stewardship of Tom Walkinshaw Racing and, for 1987, the experienced Watson was recruited as part of a three-car effort at La Sarthe, driving the XJR-8.

"[Jaguar designer] Tony Southgate embraced F1 technology by using carbon fibre. It was a high-downforce car, whereas the Porsche used an aluminium tub and a flat-six motor, so in a sprint configuration it couldn't generate the level of downforce that the Jaguar could. Part of that was because the Jaguar had a V12 motor, which was relatively narrow but very tall. The downside of this was that it had a very high centre of gravity, though it enabled the designer to build very large aero tunnels.

"We won every [World Sportscar Championship] race up to Le Mans, because ours was a better sprint car than the Porsche," explained Watson, who shared wins with Jan Lammers at Jarama and Monza, while the sister car of Eddie Cheever/Raul Boesel took top spot at Jerez and Silverstone. "The Porsche arguably had a better and more powerful motor, but it's all about lap time and the Jaguar was more like a F1 car in that respect," he added.

No luck at Le Mans

"When we went to Le Mans that year, they were still running the original layout [no Mulsanne chicanes], so the team had come up with a special aero package. Part of that involved removing the rear wheel spats, which made a contribution to the downforce in the sprint car. The outcome was that it turned a very nice car – albeit a more edgy, nervy car than the Porsche – into a very unpleasant one! They'd taken away too much of the downforce and that had allowed this high centre of gravity, which was fundamentally coming from the engine, to take control. So the car was nowhere near as ⮕

Watson's two worlds collide. McLaren's engine deal with Porsche paved the way for Watson to race the works Rothmans 956. GETTY IMAGES

to try and save fuel. That led to what I understood to be a harmonic failure."

Despite the obvious disappointment of not seeing the finish, Watson has nothing but praise for what Porsche built. This is backed up by the results accrued by the 956 and its follow-up, the 962, during this period: seven successive wins between 1981 and '87, including podium lockouts from '82 through '86.

"In its context, that car was as good as anything I've ever driven," he said. "Obviously the Le Mans set-up didn't have the kind of downforce figures that a ground-effect F1 car would have had, but for me it was about having the balance so that I could drive with confidence. I always thought that was what you needed at Le Mans: a car that gave you the confidence to drive flat-out at all times; be it day, night, wet, dry – whatever. What you don't want is a nervy, twitchy car with a lot of front-end. That Porsche certainly had everything; it was just a very nice car to drive."

Enter the Big Cats. Having raced with Porsche, Watson then wound up aboard Jaguar's formidable XJR series Group C cars. This is 1988 alongside Raul Boesel and Henri Pescarolo. GETTY IMAGES

nice to drive as the Porsche and consequently Porsche won the race, because it was by far the better car for Le Mans.

"In 1987 I was with Jan Lammers, and Win Percy was brought in as the third driver for Le Mans. He was a big mate of Tom Walkinshaw and very accomplished. During the evening, driving down the Mulsanne and approaching the kink, one of the rear tyres let go at over 200mph. The car was thrown upside down – it was a massive, massive accident – but Win stepped out of it totally uninjured. The reason he was able to do so was that the carbon fibre chassis protected him. At the point where the accident began, he must have been doing 230mph..."

Jaguar won eight out of the 10 World Sportscar Championship races that year, giving Raul Boesel the world title while Watson/Lammers finished in runner-up spot. Yet it was Porsche that took home the win that really mattered, earning an unprecedented seventh Le Mans victory on the bounce. Jaguar went to work on ensuring that the cars were quick when it mattered the following year.

"In '88 we had a revised Le Mans package," said Watson of what was now the XJR-9. "It was much better and gave us more downforce. In terms of performance and lap time there was little to choose between the Jaguar and the Porsche. It was perhaps just in qualifying that the Porsche could use its boost to generate a little more speed, but the two were pretty equally matched when it came to race-pace. I'd still say that, of the two, the Porsche was the more comfortable to drive, though the '88 Jaguar was a much better car than we had the previous year. It proved as much by winning the race."

Indeed, despite a nervous final few hours as it nursed a barely functioning gearbox, the Jaguar of Lammers/Dumfries/Wallace secured a famous victory that ended Porsche's

Most of Watson's Group C success took place in the World Sportscar Championship. Here he waves to the Spanish crowds after winning the first round of 1987 at Jarama alongside Jan Lammers (left). They'd win twice more to finish second in the points for Jaguar. GETTY IMAGES

seven-year winning streak at Le Mans. But it was disappointment yet again for Watson – his race ended before midnight, the gearbox on his XJR-9 not proving quite so durable. Yet in a way, it would be that car's retirement that would inform Lammers of the growing gearbox issue on his own car, allowing him to make the key decision that would win Jaguar the race. Fate has a funny way of presenting itself at Le Mans.

Strength in numbers

"In 1988 I was with Henri Pescarolo and Raul Boesel. Jaguar entered five cars, so there were 15 drivers in total. I'd known Henri a long while and obviously he was a legend at Le Mans; putting him in a car was massive publicity for Jaguar. I don't think our car was seen as being the quickest of the five, but if you have that many entries you'll have some that are the hares and some that are the hounds.

"For example, when Richard Attwood won for Porsche in 1970, that car was not by any

Jaguar's XJR-9 LM was a great sprint car, thanks to its superior downforce over the Porsche, and hulking V12 engine. GETTY IMAGES

For 1988, Jaguar entered a huge five cars at Le Mans and would finally earn victory at La Sarthe in the Group C age. Ironically, it was the retirement of Watson's car that helped inform the winners. GETTY IMAGES

stretch of the imagination the quickest in the race, but it was the one that took the chequered flag. That was the thinking behind Jaguar having five cars – it was a case of strength in numbers. If the front-runner drops out, you've got your backups."

In 1989 Watson switched camps again, joining Japanese marque Toyota to drive its 89C-V at Le Mans and a handful of other World Sportscar Championship events. The machinery may not have been as remarkable as what he'd experienced previously at La Sarthe, but Watson is generally positive about the car. Instead, his abiding memory of being part of the Toyota team experience is more about cross-cultural relations.

"This was the first time I'd driven for a Japanese team and I came to see a fundamental cultural difference," he explained. "I did Le Mans with them in '89 as well as some sprint races and I remember at one stage we went to the management and said: 'Our principal competitors are running Michelin tyres; we're on Bridgestones, but we need to be on Michelins too, they're quicker.' The team said, 'No, we won't do that, we have a contract with Bridgestone and we honour our commitments.' They weren't prepared to do what a European team might have done.

"The Japanese do things their way. They've got a five-year plan where they build towards achieving their goal, whereas a European team will usually look to achieve its goal at the earliest opportunity. They don't operate on a five-year plan because they're usually privateers like TWR, operating on behalf of a manufacturer. Tom Walkinshaw made the judgements, not Jaguar, whereas with Toyota everything had to be referred back to Japan."

As for the race, Watson was once again free to spend Saturday night at his leisure. On this occasion, one of his co-drivers spun approaching the Ford chicane and damaged the Toyota's rear, ending their effort with just 58 laps in the books. For those keeping count, Watson was now on a run of six successive retirements at La Sarthe, not especially remarkable during the days of high attrition but frustrating all the same. For 1990, he would return for what proved to be one final roll of ➲

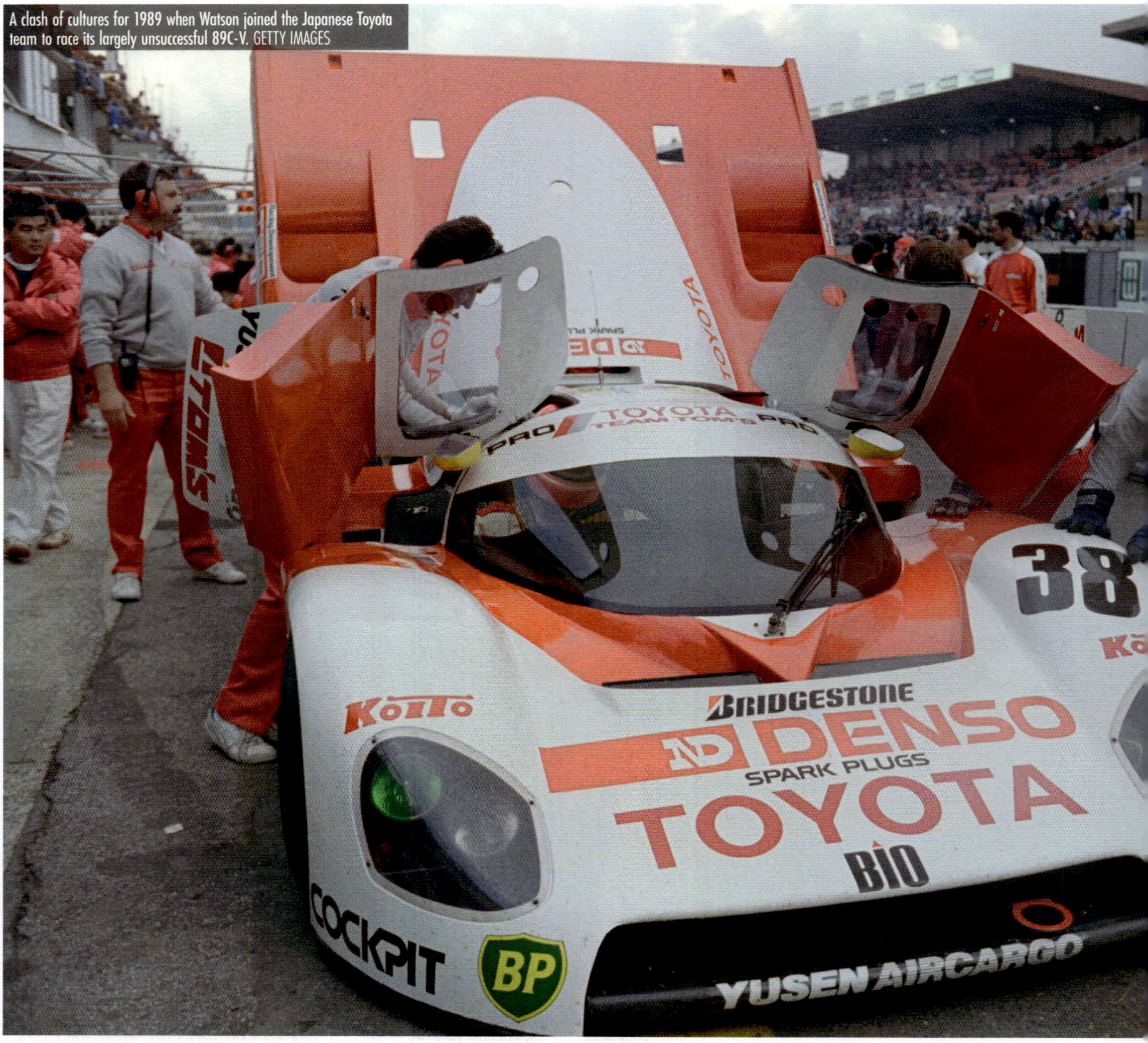

A clash of cultures for 1989 when Watson joined the Japanese Toyota team to race its largely unsuccessful 89C-V. GETTY IMAGES

A final fling with Porsche in 1990. The 'fetching pink' 962 was one of the last customer cars, and finally delivered a Le Mans finish. GETTY IMAGES

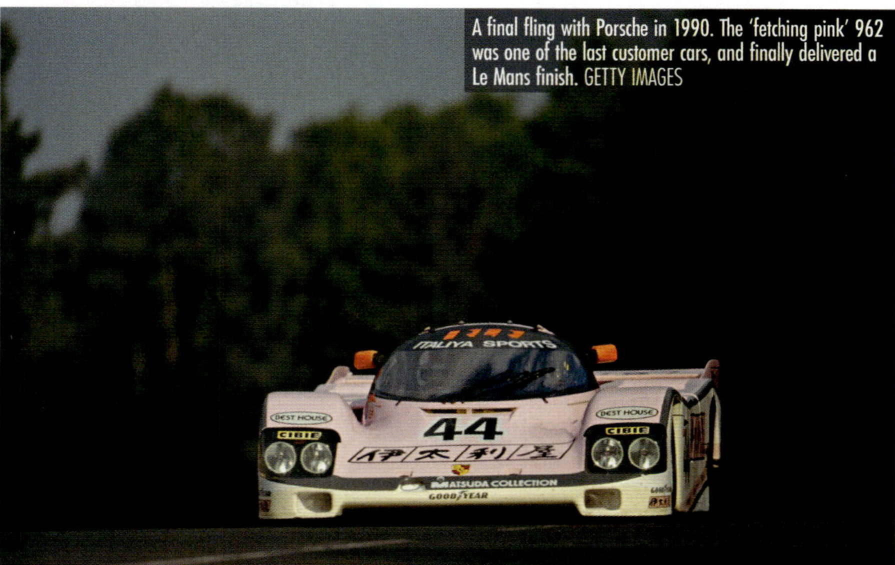

the dice, driving a privateer 962 with Allen Berg and Bruno Giacomelli.

Rock star car

"I think [Pink Floyd drummer] Nick Mason may have owned that car, but it was run by Richard Lloyd Racing and sponsored by a Japanese company, which meant it was painted a very fetching pink," recalled Watson. "It was a bog-standard, out-of-the-box 962, one of the last customer cars delivered I believe. There'd been a major circuit revision by this point whereby the ACO added chicanes on the Mulsanne, which limited the top speeds by quite a lot. Our pink Porsche was delivered in long-tail configuration and, as it turned out, the shorter tail worked much better.

"While it wasn't quite as quick on the straight, it was much better over the lap. The private Porsches were mostly long-tail, while the factory cars and the very quick

Across his sportscar career, Watson shared with many illustrious team-mates, such as Stefan Bellof, Henri Pescarolo and Mike Hailwood. GETTY IMAGES

independents were short-tail. So ours wasn't especially competitive, though again it was a nice car to drive. It was well-balanced and it didn't put too much physical or mental strain upon the driver."

Most importantly of all, this one got to the finish. So, while TWR gave Jaguar its second win in three years, the pink Porsche came home 11th to finally end Watson's run of misfortune at La Sarthe.

"It was only then I fully appreciated what the event was all about," he said. "I used to joke that Le Mans was 22 hours too long, but when you finish it, there is a great sense of achievement. Nowadays it's 24 one-hour sprint races – a totally different race compared with those I was competing in during the 80s. There's no question that there was hard racing back then, but with the evolution of technology and engineering, these cars can now lap at very high speeds for a long time."

As to whether he'll follow the centenary edition, Watson has eyes only for the Porsche contingent. Not only does he retain a deep affection for the Stuttgart brand, the new Multimatic-built 963 LMDh challenger will be run by Watson's former boss, Roger Penske.

"I am a dyed in the wool Porsche fan," he confirmed. "For me, it was the fulfilment of a childhood dream to race a factory Porsche at Le Mans. Now, the factory Porsches I wanted to race were the cars of the 50s and early 60s, but I still feel very privileged to have driven the Group C cars."

While Watson may not have driven the Porsches of his own childhood dreams, he did get to tackle Le Mans in the era-defining eighties equivalent – not to mention Jaguar's own iconic effort. For those raised on a diet of Group C beasts slugging it out at La Sarthe, that really is the stuff of fantasy. ●

Across seven Le Mans starts between 1973 and 1990, Watson drove for four different manufacturers, before finishing his La Sarthe career in the Richard Lloyd Porsche 962C. GETTY IMAGES

MAZDA'S ROTARY MAGIC

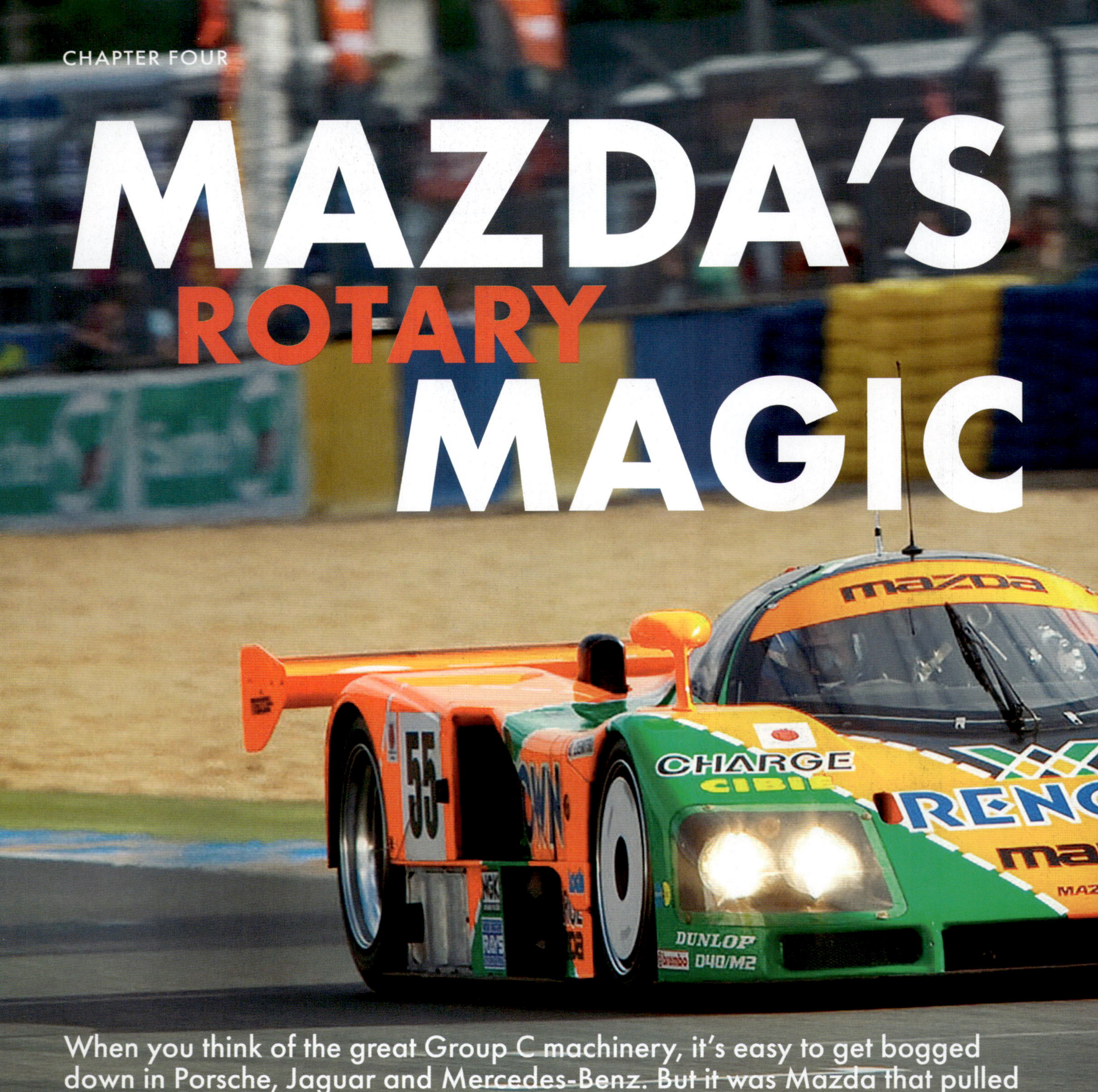

When you think of the great Group C machinery, it's easy to get bogged down in Porsche, Jaguar and Mercedes-Benz. But it was Mazda that pulled off the biggest shock of the formula with its wonderful 787B screamer.

Ask Johnny Herbert what was special about the Mazda 787B and you'll get a fairly non-descript answer, except for a single point: "There was no one thing, it was the entire package that we had, with the team, the drivers, the strategy... but there was that engine... silky smooth, perhaps the best I've ever driven. And that noise, of course!"

Herbert's last comment likely still resonates with anybody who witnessed the 1991 Le Mans 24 Hours. The banshee-like wail of the Mazda 787B was one of, and perhaps even *the*, definitive Le Mans soundtrack. Many still eulogise about the symphony of its 9,000rpm rotary engine echoing down the Mulsanne.

But the character of the 787B goes way deeper than just what we could hear. This car made history in many ways – the first Japanese car to win Le Mans outright, while also being the first to do so without a conventional reciprocating piston engine design. Plus, it had a Le Mans legend in its corner, and Herbert – a British underdog hero – in the cockpit. The 787B emerged victorious against the odds on what was its last-chance saloon. Those factors combine to make the 787B one of the most endearing Le Mans success stories.

Rotary or 'Wankel' power was nothing new to Mazda, which had been pioneering its piston-less engine technology in racing as far back as the 1960s. The original Mazda Cosmo

made a statement about the reliability of the concept by finishing fourth in the gruelling 1968 Marathon de la Route event at the Nürburgring, essentially an 84-hour thrash that ran cars to breaking point. Yet the diminutive roadster with its 982cc engine came through it with aplomb, leading Mazda to think that when it came to endurance racing, there was something in this.

It would be similar longevity that would be at the heart of the 787B's success over two decades later. Mazda continued to refine its rotary racing engines through various GT programmes before entering Group C for 1983 with the fairly underwhelming 717C. Back then Mazda stuck to a 1,300cc two-rotor engine, similar in construction to its road-going unit.

Drivers competed to find the best fuel efficiency from their driving. MAZDA

Mazda's 787B made Le Mans history for a number of reasons, including being the first Japanese winner. MAZDA

But it became clear pretty fast that development would be needed.

Fast forward to 1990 and the 787 arrived – Mazda's sixth prototype effort. Designed by Nigel Stroud, it was built around a carbon-Kevlar monocoque, with a new, expanded 2,616cc quad-rotor powerplant nestled behind it. The engine now also featured three spark plugs per rotor, but even then it didn't boast the sort of performance to trouble big-hitters like Porsche, Jaguar and Mercedes-Benz. At its first Le Mans, the lead car lapped some 16 seconds slower than the pole-sitting Nissan R90CK and finished the race 20th, 55 laps down on the winning TWR Jaguar XJR-12.

With Group C's engine regulations due to be restricted from 1992 to those using Formula 1-style 3.5-litre units only, 1991 would be Mazda's very last shot with a rotary – and it didn't waste it.

Back to the drawing board

Mazdaspeed's engineers made as many as 80 changes to the engine that went into the tweaked 787B, a key one being variable length telescopic intake runners, which would be controlled automatically by the car's ECU ➲

The 787B may not have been the fastest, but it proved the most reliable at Le Mans. MAZDA

The drivers: L-R: Bertrand Gachot, Volker Weidler and Johnny Herbert. MAZDA

and effectively smooth out the engine's torque curve, so full power would be available at far fewer revs.

By now, the 787B was capable of producing around 900bhp in fully unleashed qualifying trim, although to save fuel the engine was restricted to 8,500rpm for the race. Mazda would be playing a tortoise and hare game, after all. And to top everything off, Mazda employed Le Mans hero Jacky Ickx to act as adviser to the programme and the famed Belgian had an immediate impact, persuading the rule makers that the 787B should be allowed to run without the additional ballast being thrown at other

'old-spec' Group C cars for continuing to run old-style engines. So, while the TWR Jags and Porsche 962s were laden to 1,000kg, the 787B tipped the scales at just 830kg.

For Le Mans, three cars were entered, but they weren't fancied. With a sixth place in the opening World Sportscar Championship round at Suzuka being the 787B's best result to date, it was clear it needed a miracle to be able to compete over 24 hours.

"There's no way we were the favourites for Le Mans that year," said Herbert, who shared the green and orange number 55 car with Belgian Bertrand Gachot and German Volker

Weidler. "We knew we couldn't compete on single-lap pace and sure enough we were well off it in qualifying, but we knew we had a car we could push for every lap, such was the reliability. That, and fuel-saving would be the key for us.

"It was a competition between the drivers of not just how fast we could go, but how fast we could go while keeping that fuel usage number down and we had that competition every time we got in the car. Although we had to push as hard as we could, that fuel number was so important for the strategy."

Come qualifying and Mercedes-Benz's then-young hotshot Michael Schumacher put the C11 on top, 12 seconds quicker than the #55 787B. But come the race, the hare began to falter.

With the extra weight, both the Jaguars and Porsches struggled for fuel mileage and then the odds-on favourite Mercedes featuring Schumacher suffered a serious gearbox issue. Another Mercedes dropped out when driver Stanley Dickens ran over debris that damaged the car's floor and crankshaft and then the final C11's water pump packed up.

That left the Mazda in the lead and Herbert at the wheel and showing impressive pace, especially so considering he was still badly afflicted by the career-threatening leg injuries he sustained in a Formula 3000 crash at Brands Hatch just three years earlier.

Regardless, Ickx asked Herbert to stay in the car, knowing he had the measure of both the fuel saving and the consistent pace Mazda needed.

Victory, but no podium

"The 787B was actually really easy to drive," said Herbert. "It was so smooth, with a very long, flat power band that you could ease on and off without spinning the wheels or anything like that.

The 1991 podium, without Herbert after he collapsed having finishing the race. MAZDA

It was also very comfortable, considering it was a racing car, it was never aggressive to drive. So when I was asked to extend my stint, I just did it.

"The team decided it would be silly to put somebody else in the car when I was in the groove. But my drinks bottle got used up in my first stint and it was a very hot afternoon and really, really hot inside the car... at the end my head was spinning."

Herbert crossed the line with a two-lap advantage over the best of the Jaguars, but even then the drama wasn't done. Using the last of his strength to lever himself out of the car, Herbert promptly collapsed from dehydration and never made it to the podium, leaving Gachot and Wiedler to celebrate between themselves as Herbert got medical attention.

"I collapsed over the bonnet, apparently," said Herbert. "They took me to the medical centre to get some fluids into me, so I missed the podium. But I was fit for the party later though!" Hydration certainly wouldn't have been a problem there. ●

The Wankel engine, capable of producing 900bhp. MAZDA

Unfancied against the faster Jaguars, Mazda pulled off one of the greatest all-time Le Mans shocks MAZDA

INTO THE
MODERN DAY

And so, to more familiar territory. After the fall of the Group C monsters, brute force gave way to delicate precision as Le Mans became home to the most advanced racing prototypes anywhere in the world.

With Group C in its death throes, something had to change to rejuvenate Le Mans' top tier. It may have taken a convoluted trial-and-error process to get there, but the advent of the Le Mans Prototype classes established a template that would endure for over 20 years and set the standard for the modern race we all know and love.

The clearly defined four-category format – LMP1, LMP2, GTE Pro and GTE Am – has provided the main classes at the Le Mans 24 Hours since 2004 and laid the framework for driver progression in the modern day, with LMP1 operating strictly for professionals and the smaller LMP2 class for crews with mixed abilities. Ditto for the twin GT categories.

Key Moments

1995 McLaren makes the most successful Le Mans debut ever with the F1 GTR

1997 Tom Kristensen makes his Le Mans debut, and wins...

2003 Bentley secures its first victory since 1930 with the Speed 8

2005 Audi's R8 takes its fifth win to become the most successful Le Mans car of all-time

2006 Audi brings diesel power to Le Mans with the R10 TDI, Peugeot joins in 2007

2010 Audi sets a new race distance record, with the winning R15+ TDI covering 5410.7km, 397 laps

2012 Toyota returns to the sport, buoyed by new hybrid rules

2013 Tom Kristensen takes his ninth, and final, Le Mans win. He retires after 2014.

2017 Porsche secures its final victory of the LMP1 era, stretching its all-time record to 19. Kamui Kobayashi sets a new lap record in qualifying in his Toyota TS050 Hybrid, a 3m14.791s (156.5mph average)

2020 The final race to run for the LMP1 ruleset

The LMP1 rule set reached its absolute high in 2015 when both manufacturer interest and hybrid power were at their peak at Le Mans. PORSCHE

LMP1 brought with it some stunning feats of engineering, as well as producing the most successful single model ever to race at Le Mans, Audi's evergreen R8. Although it was technically born when the top tier was clunkily named LMP900, in deference to weight limits, the R8 was an LMP1 car through and through and would go on to record five outright victories, toppling cars such as Ford's GT40, Porsche's 956, and the Alfa Romeo 8Cs that led the way pre-WWII.

The LMP1 era resulted in tumbling lap and distance records as technology redefined what a racing car could do at Le Mans. The first cars began to appear in 1992, but due to an ever-changing process of class titles and rule tweaking (from LMWSC, via LMGTP and LMP900), it would eventually take 12 years for the now-familiar format to take shape.

GTs rule the roost

While prototype racing appeared to be in a constant state of flux during the mid 1990s, with Group C gone and LMP rules in their infancy, Le Mans enjoyed a short period of success with GT cars, namely the McLaren F1 GTR and Porsche's 911 GT1.

McLaren arrived for 1995 and took La Sarthe by storm. The F1 GTR model was not originally destined for racing, yet it would go on to prove itself more than adept by recording not only ⮑

The Winners

1995
McLaren F1 GTR
Yannick Dalmas/Masanori Sekiya/JJ Lehto, 4056km

1996
TWR Porsche WSC-95
Davy Jones/Alexander Wurz/Manuel Reuter, 4814km

1997
TWR Porsche WSC-95
Michele Alboreto/Stefan Johansson/Tom Kristensen, 4910km

1998
Porsche 911 GT1-98
Laurent Aïello/Allan McNish/Stéphane Ortelli, 4784km

1999
BMW V12 LMR
Joachim Winkelhock/Pierluigi Martini/Yannick Dalmas, 4983km

2000
Audi R8
Frank Biela/Tom Kristensen/Emanuele Pirro, 5008km

2001
Audi R8
Frank Biela/Tom Kristensen/Emanuele Pirro, 4367km

2002
Audi R8
Frank Biela/Tom Kristensen/Emanuele Pirro, 5119km

2003
Bentley Speed 8
Rinaldo Capello/Guy Smith/Tom Kristensen, 5146km

2004
Audi R8
Seiji Ara/Rinaldo Capello/Tom Kristensen, 5170km

2005
Audi R8
Tom Kristensen/JJ Lehto/Marco Werner, 5051km

2006
Audi R10 TDI
Frank Biela/Marco Werner/Emanuele Pirro, 5187km

2007
Audi R10 TDI Marco
Marco Werner/Emanuele Pirro/Frank Biela, 5029km

2008
Audi R10 TDI
Allan McNish/Rinaldo Capello/Tom Kristensen, 5193km

2009
Peugeot 908 HDi FAP
David Brabham/Marc Gené/Alexander Wurz, 5206km

2010
Audi R15 TDI Plus
Mike Rockenfeller/Timo Bernhard/Romain Dumas, 5411km

2011
Audi R18 TDI
Marcel Fässler/André Lotterer/Benoît Tréluyer, 4838km

2012
Audi R18 e-tron quattro
Marcel Fässler/André Lotterer/Benoît Tréluyer, 5152km

2013
Audi R18 e-tron quattro
Loïc Duval, Tom Kristensen, Allan McNish, 4742.9km

2014
Audi R18 e-tron quattro
Marcel Fässler, Benoît Treluyer, André Lotterer, 5165.4km

2015
Porsche 919 Hybrid.
Earl Bamber, Nico Hülkenberg, Nick Tandy, 5382.8km

2016
Porsche 919 Hybrid
Romain Dumas, Neel Jani, Marc Lieb, 5233.5km

2017
Porsche 919 Hybrid
Earl Bamber, Timo Bernhard, Brendon Hartley, 5001.2km

2018
Toyota TS050 Hybrid
Fernando Alonso, Sébastien Buemi, Kazuki Nakajima, 5286.8km

2019
Toyota TS050 Hybrid
Fernando Alonso, Sébastien Buemi, Kazuki Nakajima, 5246km

2020
Toyota TS050 Hybrid
Sébastien Buemi, Brendon Hartley, Kazuki Nakajima, 5272.5km

2021
Toyota GR010 Hybrid
Mike Conway, Kamui Kobayashi, José María López, 5054.5km

2022
Toyota GR010 Hybrid
Sébastien Buemi, Brendon Hartley, Ryo Hirakawa, 5177.1km

Aston Martin has been hugely successful in the GT classes of the race, with first its DBR9 GT1 and then Vantage GTE models. This is its GTE Pro win in 2020. ASTON MARTIN RACING

one of the biggest shock results in the race's history, but also the most successful Le Mans debut of all time. More on that later…

Then, during the peak of the revival of international GT racing with the BPR Global GT Series, brands began to push the envelope with what they could legally claim to be road-derived grand touring cars. Porsche's 911 GT1 was the ultimate case. Designed first and foremost as a racing prototype in GT clothing, a few road-going versions were knocked out purely for homologation purposes and the cars swept the board in the BPR Series, which would eventually morph into the FIA GT Championship.

But while Porsche's 911 GT1 was ruling shorter races, the Stuttgart brand hedged its bets by also creating a new prototype for Le Mans in 1996, which would inadvertently give Group C one final unofficial hurrah. Porsche struck a deal with Tom Walkinshaw to build a new car using the plans for the Jaguar XJR-14. Shorn of its roof, the Ross Brawn and John Piper-designed chassis was modified to accept Porsche's 3-litre turbocharged flat-six 935 engine, and the TWR Porsche WSC-95 was born.

Only two cars were ever built and Joest Racing's model managed to pip the best of the 911 GT1s by a single lap in 1996, with Davy Jones, Manuel Reuter and Alexander Wurz winning. Wurz, aged just 22 years and 91 days, would become Le Mans' youngest-ever outright winner – a record that still stands.

The WSC-95 would triumph once again in 1997, this time carrying a driver who would go on to become the greatest ever at the race. Tom Kristensen was chasing his Formula 1 dream when a last-minute call came from Joest to offer him the third seat in the car alongside Michele Alboreto and Stefan Johansson for 1997.

"At first I wasn't all that keen," remembered Kristensen. "I visited the workshops to see if I would even be comfortable in the car. I sat in it and felt at home immediately. I remember saying to Reinhold [Joest] that it would be perfect if we could move the brake a few millimetres forward and I remember him leaning over and saying to me: 'Our fastest driver decides that'. It put me firmly in my place!"

Yet it would be Kristensen who became that fastest driver. During the night-time stint, his pace was such that Joest simply left him out longer and longer, the Dane repeatedly shattering the lap record on his first appearance

as the car ran on to victory. It would be the first of Kristensen's incredible nine visits to the top step of the Le Mans podium.

With the WSC shelved for 1998, GT1 took its turn in the sun as Allan McNish/ Laurent Aiello/Stéphane Ortelli led a comfortable one-two for Porsche ahead of the Nissan R390s.

Prototype racing's rise would begin properly a year later, when BMW's V12 LMR would show the way, with Joachim Winkelhock/Pierluigi Martini/Yannick Dalmas proving the class of the field. A new development partnership with the Williams F1 team helped hone the V12 LMR's aero, while the S70 V12 engine that had powered the McLaren F1 did the rest.

Mercedes flips out

That 1999 race was also memorable for Mercedes' high-profile, and somewhat high-flying, issues with its CLR GT1s. The CLR was hugely fast, but its short-wheelbase design with long overhanging bodywork had a fundamental flaw. While fine on smooth-as-glass permanent circuits where its aerodynamics could suck it to the track and help generate incredible cornering speeds, on the bumps of La Sarthe air could gush under the car and produce catastrophic lift at high speeds.

First Mark Webber's car flipped at Indianapolis on Thursday night, prompting the team to do a full rebuild and analysis ahead of the weekend. A call to McLaren's Adrian Newey – then on duty with the F1 team at the Canadian Grand Prix – produced a solution of fitting dive planes in an attempt to boost the frontal downforce. But even that didn't stop Webber's car taking another tumble

The start of the 2012 race. With no Peugeot to play with, Audi beat the returning Toyotas with its R18 e-tron quattro. AUDI SPORT

The only break in Audi's early dominance came when Bentley made a breakthrough in 2003, and even that was a VW Group-backed entry. BENTLEY

The rise of GT1 cars in the mid 1990s produced the formidable Porsche 911 GT1, which ran away with the race in 1998. PORSCHE AG

Oh dear, at least they had a go! The much-unloved, but very unusual Nissan GT-R LM Nismo. The project only appeared for 2015 and wasn't great. NISSAN

during Saturday morning warm-up, putting the machine out for good.

The drivers were consulted over whether or not they thought the cars were safe to race, and Briton Peter Dumbreck recalled: "We were never going to say no. We were racing drivers and we just got on with it. We were told to lift off the throttle to control the speeds at key points around the lap, like the Mulsanne and Indianapolis, but even that didn't help."

A few hours into the race and Dumbreck's car took off at terrifying speed just before Indianapolis. "I just remember seeing sky, track, sky, trees…" said Dumbreck, who escaped from the wreck without injury. "They put me on a stretcher and were telling me to stay still but I was moving my arms and legs to check they all still worked."

Mercedes withdrew the final car and has never returned to Le Mans since. And, to rub salt in the wounds, because Dumbreck's accident took place on what is legally public road, the police even insisted on breathalysing him.

Audi's sleeping giant awakens

Another car in the field that year caused what was arguably an even bigger impact. Audi's formative Dallara-built R8R may not have set the world alight with its run to third place, but it had far wider reaching impact by spawning the all-conquering R8 of 2000.

Running both an open-topped car and a closed-cockpit R8C that year as a sort of rolling aero experiment gave Audi all the data it needed to develop its next challenger. Backed by a healthy budget from the Volkswagen Group and developed in partnership with Joest Racing, the R8 was like nothing that had been seen before at Le Mans. Boasting a carbon chassis that was designed so that entire sections of the car could be unbolted and replaced as full assemblies – like a Lego model – it took endurance racing efficiency to a whole new level. Joest once changed an entire rear-end assembly in just over three minutes, gearbox and all, something that would have normally taken a few hours.

As the sole major manufacturer in the field, the R8 steam-rollered its way to a podium whitewash on its debut in 2000 and then simply didn't stop winning. Audi monopolised Le Mans for the next three years, its winning streak only interrupted by another VW-owned brand, Bentley in 2003 – and even that had Audi DNA.

Racing Technology Norfolk (RTN) took the core of the R8C and breathed new life into it, modifying the twin-turbo Audi V8 to 4.0-litres capacity and making sweeping aero changes by raising the height of the nose and creating new channels through the body for the air to flow.

Bentley's return came in 2001, ending an 86-year hiatus, with one of the EXP Speed 8s scoring a podium and then a fourth the next year. But for 2003, Bentley would throw everything at it, running the car in America to gain mileage, adopting the same Michelin tyres as Audi, and even making use of the same team, with Joest Racing recruited to run the car in the absence of Audi's works effort, which was taking its own sabbatical.

Bentley started on pole and led practically the entire event with Kristensen/Rinaldo Capello/Guy Smith scoring the British marque its first Le Mans success since 1930. Job done in year three, the plug was pulled and Bentley walked away again, with no return in sight.

With Audi's works team still off focusing on road car sales and the Bentleys now tucked up as museum pieces, it fell to Japan's Team Goh to uphold honour, wheeling its customer R8 to victory in 2004, before Champion Racing did likewise a year later. Kristensen was at the heart of both projects as he kept up his incredible winning streak in the 2000s, scorching to six-straight victories. In doing so, he ensured a record of five from six for the R8, before its rather controversial successor arrived.

Here's to the oil-burners

The R10 TDI made huge headlines when it was first unveiled. A dirty diesel, at Le Mans? Surely not! ➲

Porsche's moment of glory in 2015, which was *the* race to win of the LMP1 era. PORSCHE AG

Porsche's winning crew of 2015 L-R: Nick Tandy, Earl Bamber and Nico Hülkenberg, of F1 fame. PORSCHE AG

In fact, diesel had first appeared in the race way back in 1949, although it didn't fare too well. But in this new era of efficiency and government pushes toward the benefits of diesel mileage, Audi went for it, developing the R10 to be based on the R8's chassis and aerodynamic principles, but with an all-new 5.5-litre turbocharged diesel V12 at its heart.

As explained further in this issue, drivers were initially blown away by the car's mountainous torque, which initially proved a problem for the differentials to handle. The R10 made a winning debut in 2006 as Audi began to look unstoppable, but a new rivalry dawned when Peugeot announced its own diesel-powered effort for 2007. While the new 908 HDi FAP proved rapid in qualifying, it couldn't match the Audi's consistency, the best finishing second, some 10 laps down on the winning R10 that year. And so a pattern began to emerge – Peugeot would often be the king of qualifying, whereas Audi got the job done in the race.

Peugeot should have won easily in 2008, outpacing the older Audis by almost six seconds per lap, but the team's challenge crumbled thanks to a combination of heavy rain better suiting the Audis and ill-advised bodywork changes causing overheating.

Peugeot would finally break through in 2009, securing a one-two despite some early race fumbles in the pits. But that would be its high point. After taking a battering from Audi's new R15 in 2010, it would miss a second win by just 14 seconds in 2011 and then shut up shop amid financial difficulties on the road car side.

Return of the big hitters

That left Audi to face off against a fledgling programme from Toyota, which had been lured

back thanks to the introduction of new hybrid powertrain rules for LMP1. However, the rivalry never kicked off as much as its fight with Peugeot had. The Ingolstadt marque would stretch its unbeaten run at Le Mans to a further five, before LMP1 reached its all-time high in 2015.

Another brand keen to jump on the hybrid bandwagon was Porsche. Its new 919 Hybrid made its Le Mans debut in 2014 but was only half-baked. It did briefly lead the race for the first time since 1998, but it wound up a long way behind Audi and Toyota.

But, come 2015, it was a different story. With three years of development under the hybrid rules, the cars were creating obscene levels of performance. Many drivers likened

the sensation of racing the new turbocharged petrol-electric monsters to being fired out of a cannon – and with reports of cars producing north of 1300bhp, it's easy to understand why.

Le Mans 2015 will go down as one of the finest duels ever witnessed in the modern age, with Audi, Toyota, Porsche and (to a lesser extent) Nissan throwing the kitchen sink at it – and it was Porsche that packed the biggest punch.

There were cynical cries of 'marketing exercise' when the wraps came off a third 919 Hybrid with F1 driver Nico Hülkenberg's name on it, alongside those of Earl Bamber and Nick Tandy. At the time flying high with Force India, Hülkenberg brought grand prix attention to endurance racing and the crew ended up being

Toyota came to the fore after Porsche ducked out following 2017. The Japanese team is now unbeaten across the last five Le Mans, including winning the first two of the new Hypercar era. TOYOTA GAZOO RACING

the darkest of dark horses – but it wasn't the German who made the difference.

After a cagey first quarter of the race with Audi, a spectacular quadruple stint from British star Tandy through the depths of the night turned the tide in the Porsche's favour.

"The thing I remember most from that race weekend, and I recall it so vividly... I was sat in the garage getting ready to go in for another stint, and it was about 11pm. Nico was in the car and it had got cool and the dark had come in and it suited our car and we suddenly became the fastest thing out there," remembered Tandy. "We'd lost some time early on, but I saw the gaps coming down and saw the performance of the car in those conditions and I watched the screen for a good 30 minutes, knowing I was going in soon and thinking: 'My god, this is potentially our chance. Right now we have a chance to win this race'.

"I said to myself there and then, 'You're going to get in that car and blow everybody away, you have to...' And from that moment on I was so focused, I'm not sure I've ever felt that focused, but that was it. I took the lead around 1am and never looked back."

Tandy, Bamber and Hülkenberg's car took the win by a clear lap from the sister crew of Timo Bernhard/Brendon Hartley/Mark Webber, with the Audis a further lap or two adrift and the lead Toyota sixth. It was a remarkable result for a crew that were largely written off before they even started.

"I think it was actually a good thing as Nico took the spotlight," added Tandy. "It left me with more time to concentrate on my job and deliver the goods in the car for Porsche. We knew full well there would be an extra interest in our car. And that year was amazing, we had the full Audi crew, two strong Toyotas and even the Nissans. If I could ever pick a year to win Le Mans it would definitely be that one!"

Audi simply dominated the 2000s, becoming the race's second most successful manufacturer with 13 wins in 15 races between 2000-2014. AUDI SPORT

And what of that Nissan programme? The radical front-engined GT-R LM Nismo was beset by issues, most related to the hybrid system which never worked and therefore led to the cars repeatedly boiling their brakes without the added friction of the motor generator. Both cars retired and never saw the light of day again.

As for the hybrid rules set, it eventually killed off the LMP1 era altogether. Defeated, Audi's wider troubles began to hit home. VW's 'Dieselgate' scandal was damaging and, with the once-lauded diesel engines being demonised by governments across the world, the Group was in no mood to continue showcasing its TDI tech. The programme was dropped at late notice for 2016. Despite a new prototype being built and ready for the campaign ahead, it would never race. And so ended Audi's reign.

Porsche would go on to record a hat-trick of wins before also pulling out. The rising costs of the development race (Porsche was rumoured to be spending upwards of $100-120m per season) eventually forced manufacturers to back off and the top class limped on with pretty much just Toyota present.

The LMP1 era ended in 2020 after three dominant Toyota victories. Take nothing away from the job Toyota Gazoo Racing has done, but even the team itself will tell you it would rather be beating rival brands than competing against itself. And that wider level of competition is finally here, thanks to the dawn of the Hypercar era. ●

Toyota leads the start of the final Le Mans run to LMP1 rules in 2020. This race was also the second be run in September, delayed due to the Covid pandemic, and with no fans allowed. The only other September race was back in 1968. GETTY IMAGES

THE DOMINANT DEBUT

Believe it or not, the McLaren F1 was never intended to go racing and it was only customer pressure that ever made it happen. But when the British firm's F1 GTR arrived at Le Mans in 1995, it proved a sensation.

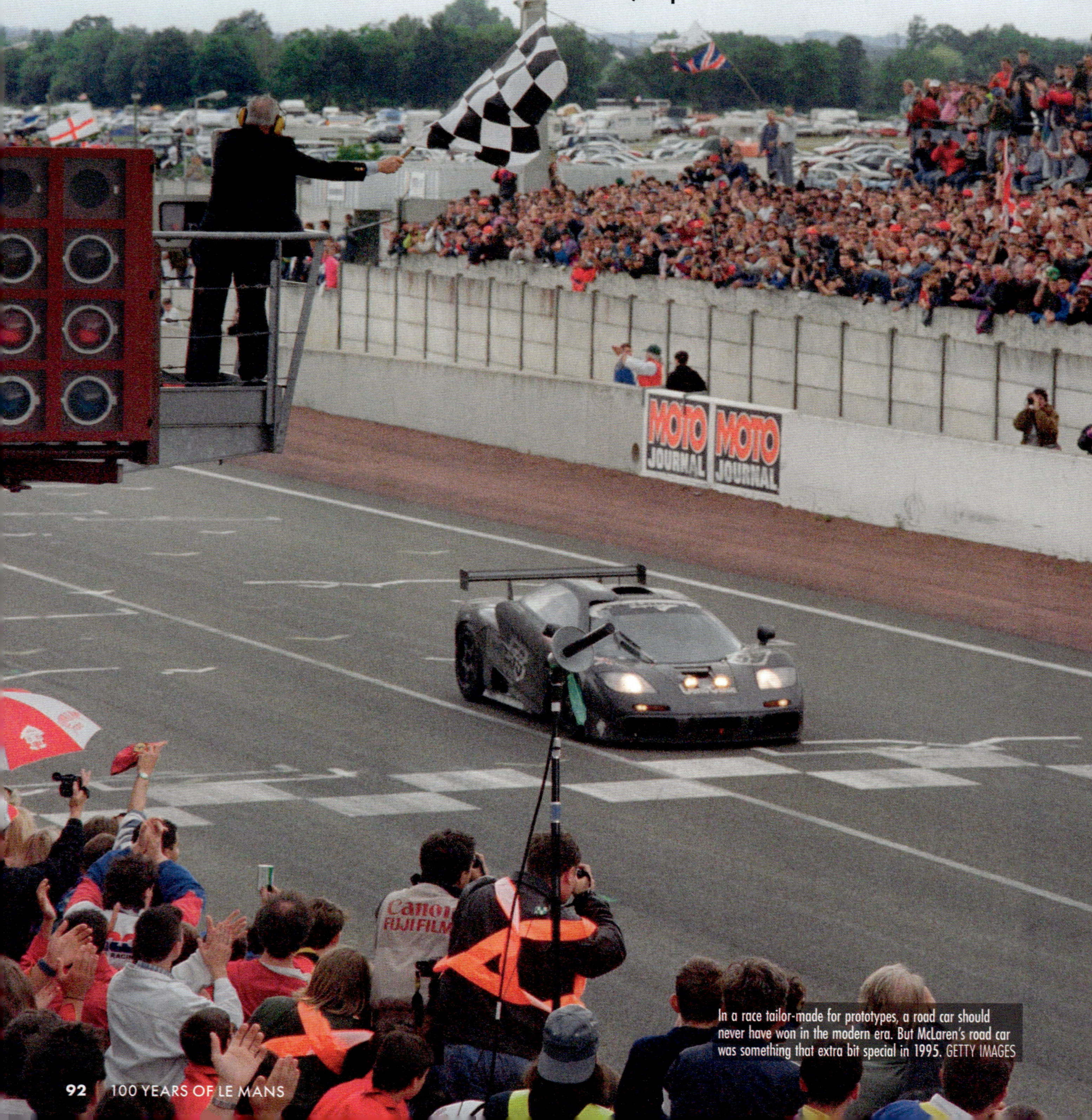

In a race tailor-made for prototypes, a road car should never have won in the modern era. But McLaren's road car was something that extra bit special in 1995. GETTY IMAGES

The list of manufacturers to have won Le Mans on their debut is surprisingly short. Just three have ever achieved the feat. Chenard and Walcker was first by default, having topped the order at the very first *Grand Prix d'Endurance*, then Ferrari became the second in 1949. But it would take 46 years for another to come along and few would have bet on it being McLaren, especially when its hopes rested on what was essentially a road car.

Admittedly, it was *some* road car. The McLaren F1 tore up the rulebook when it was first unveiled in 1992. The brainchild of Gordon Murray, the South African made the first sketches of his predominantly carbon, three-seater, V12-powered machine on a flight back from the Italian Grand Prix in 1988, successfully selling the idea to Ron Dennis that McLaren should enter the supercar market.

Such was the pedigree of the F1, its racing roots amplified by its very name, that it soon became the world's fastest production car, topping 240mph thanks to the grunt from its monster 6.1-litre BMW V12.

Yet, with all the brand's heritage and racing history, Le Mans was never the plan, as Murray explained in the documentary *McLaren at Le Mans: Pursuit of Perfection*: "When we set out to make the McLaren F1, we set out to make the ultimate road car... and that was it. The F1's direct ancestor is the line of McLaren Formula 1 racing cars. It was the world's first fully carbon road car. The whole monocoque weighed just over 100kg, just a fraction of the weight of a metal car and the engine was the most powerful naturally-aspirated unit ever made in terms of horsepower per cc. But we never, ever, intended it to go racing."

But it seemed an inevitability that it would. After years in the doldrums as manufacturers switched to costly prototypes, international GT racing was enjoying a revival at the time thanks in large to the formation of the BPR Global GT Series in 1994. Invented by now SRO Motorsport Group founder Stéphane Ratel – the godfather of modern GT racing – BPR allowed manufacturers to lightly modify their flagship sports cars and take them racing in front of big crowds for 12 rounds around the world. Road relevancy was a big draw and soon brands like Porsche, Mercedes-Benz, Ferrari and Lamborghini were churning out GT racing cars for customers again.

With a model like the McLaren F1 on the shelf, customers soon wanted to prove that their million-pound road car could cut it on the circuits too.

"When Ron and myself started to come under pressure from customers who wanted to take their F1s racing, we had to look at it as a serious project," continued Murray. "On the face of it turning a 240mph road car into a racing car sounds a simple task, but there was actually a lot more to it than we ever imagined."

Every inch covered

Along with the stringent safety requirements such as roll cage, crash protection and fire extinguishers, McLaren had to go over every inch of the F1 to prepare it for racing. The interior was stripped and the bodywork was entirely replaced to comply with regulations demanding bolt-on-bolt-off front and rear sections. Additional cooling channels had to be added and the aerodynamics reworked with new splitters, diffusers and rear wing.

But many areas were barely touched.

Details of the McLaren F1 GTR, which was never intended to go racing, but proved hugely successful. This was also chassis number 1, which went on to win Le Mans. MCLAREN

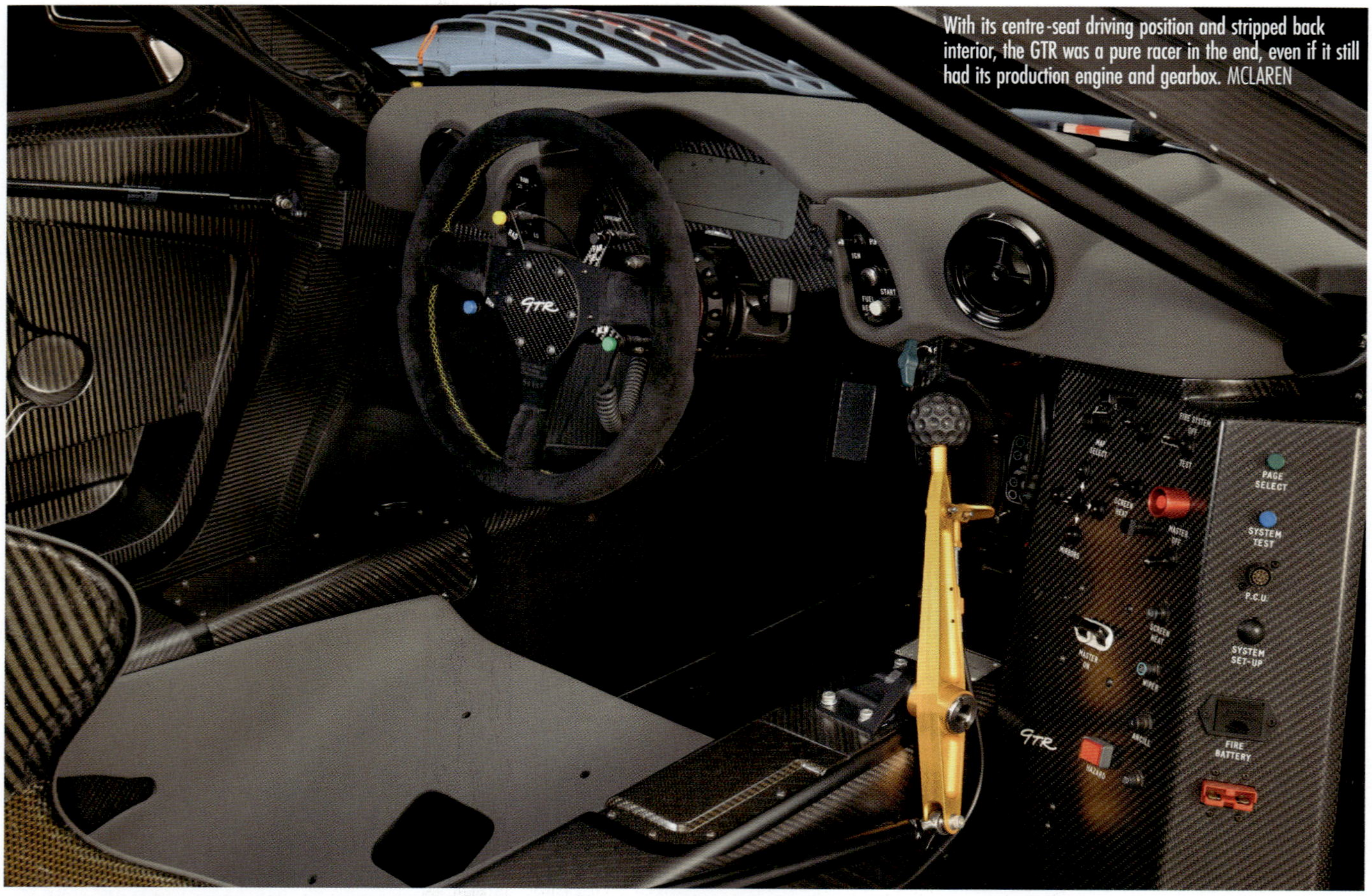

With its centre-seat driving position and stripped back interior, the GTR was a pure racer in the end, even if it still had its production engine and gearbox. MCLAREN

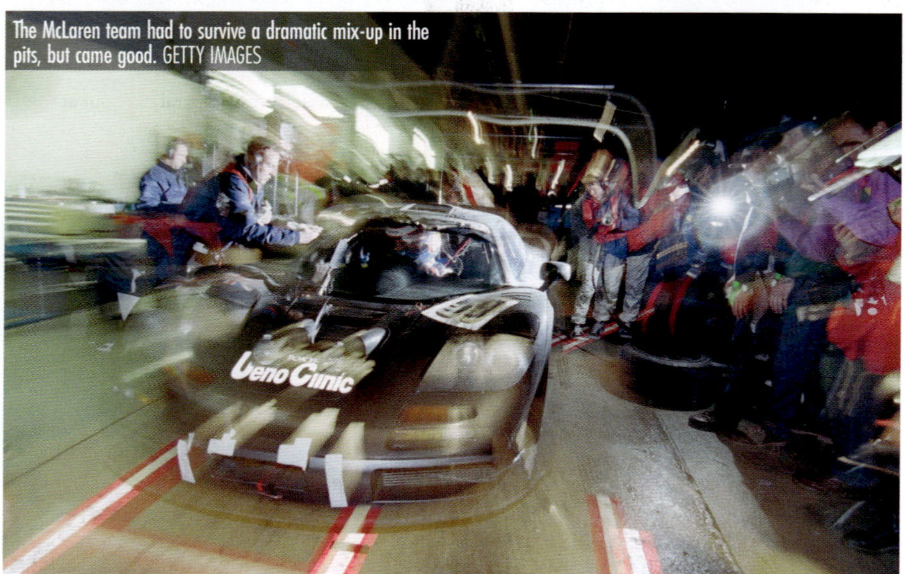

The McLaren team had to survive a dramatic mix-up in the pits, but came good. GETTY IMAGES

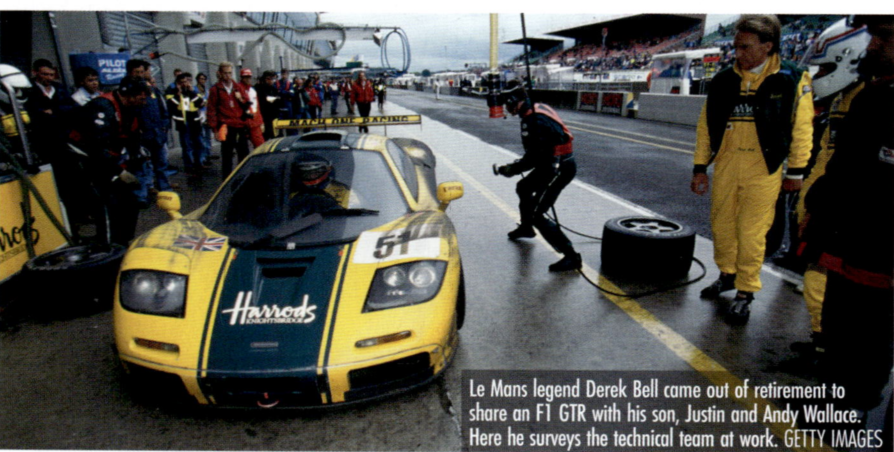

Le Mans legend Derek Bell came out of retirement to share an F1 GTR with his son, Justin and Andy Wallace. Here he surveys the technical team at work. GETTY IMAGES

The gearbox was standard, albeit with an uprated carbon clutch and the BMW V12 ran as it was, but its power was a sticking point. With GT racing restricting the output of cars to keep them all on a level playing field, an air restrictor meant the F1 GTR ended up producing around 40bhp less than the roadgoing F1. In a straight line, the F1 GTR would be some 15mph slower than its road-going variant, but cornering would be an entirely different matter.

A total of nine cars would be built for the 1995 season to race in the BPR Series, plus tackle Le Mans at their customer's request. It seemed a tall order for a completely unproven car based so roundly on a road version, but it laid the foundations for one of the great Le Mans success stories.

The clues to the F1 GTR's potential were there from the start of the year, with the car winning six of the opening seven rounds of the BPR Series before heading to Le Mans, the successes split between four wins for Ray Bellm's Gulf Racing concern and three for Thomas Bscher's West Competition outfit.

The F1 GTR's start to life was so positive that a total of seven cars would be entered for Le Mans' GT1 class that year. Gulf and West led the line with two entries each, along with the Harrods-backed Mach One Racing entry of Le Mans legend Derek Bell, his son Justin and Andy Wallace. There were GTRs from the French Giroix and BBA Compétition teams, plus one additional car few expected.

During production, McLaren had retained chassis 01, which had borne the weight of all testing and development work for the GTR project. Still in its matt black testing livery, it had never raced until the Kokusai Kaihatsu Racing team led by prolific Japanese driver

The darkest of dark horses. The test mule for the F1 GTR was only wheeled out at the last minute, but proved the best of the bunch. GETTY IMAGES

Masanori Sekiya requested one final GTR for himself, Yannick Dalmas and JJ Lehto to drive. So the test mule was prepared and rolled out. Of all the F1 GTRs, this was the most tired, yet proved to be the darkest of dark horses.

To prepare for Le Mans, McLaren had to make even more modifications to the F1. "We had to significantly upgrade the brakes from the iron ones we used for four-hour races to a new carbon-fibre set, which was essentially aircraft technology at the time," said James Robinson, head of the GTR development team. "To put into context how hard the race would be on the GTR, we're basically talking the entire

mileage of an F1 season in a single day, so the wear and tear is exceptionally high. If we'd stuck with iron brake discs, we'd need probably two changes on the front across the race and one on the rear, whereas if we were lucky we could do a race distance on the carbon ones."

Unproven, undeterred

Suitably outfitted, the F1 GTRs still faced a mammoth task. Not only had the car never competed across 24 hours before, it wasn't in the same league as the lightweight prototypes that made up the top World Sports Car (WSC) class. However, with global sports car

racing undergoing something of a reset and Le Mans' top class instead being based around IMSA rules, the WSC entry was thin at best, comprising just six cars.

Qualifying proved the point, with the fastest McLaren being just ninth and it was chassis 01 driven by Lehto. But, as team manager of the Harrods car, Dave Price, said: "We never went for a fast time in qualifying. What was the point? A total of 20 or 30 feet on the grid wasn't going to win us the race."

But what arguably would turn the tide in favour of the McLarens was the great French weather. Rain began to fall during the early stages of the race and simply didn't stop, to the point where the WSC prototypes lost their pace advantage and the lightweight open-topped cars began to fall like flies.

In contrast, the closed-cockpit McLarens were going strong, the wet weather also acting to cool and preserve their carbon brakes. It didn't mean they were easy to drive though, as Wallace related after a long stint: "When it was like that out there, I had to use all the skill I could summon just to keep the thing on the road. We were doing 200mph and skipping from puddle to puddle, getting on and off the gas trying to control it through the aquaplaning at that speed. It was scary."

For all its road-car roots, the F1 GTR was still a monster to drive. The weight of the hulking V12 behind the driver having a pendulum-like effect, not that it phased Lehto. A typically stoic Finn with immense *sisu* (inner resolve), Lehto was only just working his way back into action having suffered a broken neck during a horrific testing accident with the Benetton F1 team a year prior. Doctors warned him one more major shunt could well leave him paralysed, but at Le Mans that year he didn't seem to care. ➲

All smiles on the podium after springing a shock win. The winning drivers: L-R Masanori Sekiya, Yannick Dalmas and JJ Lehto. The Bells and Wallace are in their Harrods-liveried suits to the side. GETTY IMAGES

The F1 GTR outside McLaren's Technology Centre in Woking, scissor doors aloft. MCLAREN

"Before the race we agreed a target lap time that we'd stick to, which was 4min 10sec, but I think JJ thought he had to do that in the wet!" said manager of the Kokusai Kaihatsu entry, Paul Lanzante, who was making his first trip to Le Mans.

The McLarens weren't immune to issues. First Bellm crashed his car, then Derek Bell stopped briefly with a clutch complaint.

Lehto was put in through the night, but showed such stunning pace that by dawn the unfancied #59 GTR was second. "I know Paul had some concerns about my driving style, about being too hard on the car, but I just drove how I knew how to drive," said Lehto. "The GTR was like an F1 car with a roof. It didn't have a lot of downforce so moved about a lot on the brakes, with that big heavy engine behind you it felt like it was oversteering a lot, but I liked it. Racing it at night took full focus, especially in the wet. You drove with your eyes wide open, ready for anything, but I found it quite calming."

Back at base, and with trophies in tow. McLaren had completed the impossible and made the best Le Mans debut in history. MCLAREN

Safe to say Lanzante didn't: "At one point JJ was about 27sec faster than any other car out there, in the pouring rain, at about 3am it was quite something. When he got back into the car in the morning, I just told him to give it hell, give it all he could as the chance was there for us to win."

McLaren vs McLaren

Then, disaster struck the leading West McLaren when its clutch failed at 4am, the Kokusai Kaihatsu car found itself second, with Lehto reeling in Justin Bell's Harrods car, which had worked its way back to the head of the field after its precautionary stop.

Lehto caught and passed Bell Jr with just a few hours remaining to assume the lead, but further drama lay ahead at a seemingly routine pit stop. As the car came in, the sleep-deprived mechanics lost composure, as three wheels were taken off to be changed, the car was dropped from its jacks, landing awkwardly on its brake discs. The team recovered the situation, but the car was sent back out on the wrong tyres and would require another stop. Advantage Harrods, but only until Bell Snr brought the car back in when its clutch

The BMW factory team also got in on the act, running an F1 GTR in its own Fina works colours in 1996. MCLAREN

properly started to give out at 14:00hrs. Wallace took over but struggled to engage a gear, eventually finding a cog and managing to drag the car back into life on the starter motor. But the delay had presented the Kokusai Kaihatsu crew with the time it needed to make that extra stop to rectify its error.

Dalmas, already a two-time Le Mans winner, took over for the final stint, but had the recovering Courage C34 WSC prototype of Mario Andretti/Éric Hélary/Bob Wollek closing fast as the track dried across the final stages.

"That last hour was so tense," said Lehto. "Anything can happen and nothing can be taken for granted."

Dalmas took the flag a lap clear of the Courage, as Wallace dragged the limping Harrods McLaren home in third. To back that up, the F1 GTR that Bellm had crashed early on and had therefore lost 45 minutes to repairs came home fourth with Mark Blundell and Maurizio Sandro Sala sharing. The Giroix car completed what stands as the most successful Le Mans debut ever for a manufacturer by finishing fifth. An outright victory, and four cars within the top five. Not bad for a car that was never meant to race.

After Le Mans, the F1 GTRs would continue to sweep the board in the BPR Series, with the model winning 10 from the 12 rounds. And that wouldn't be the end of the story for the car at Le Mans. F1 GTRs would finish fourth and fifth in 1996 against much renewed competition from Porsche's regulation-bending 911 GT1 prototype. Team Gulf would take second ahead of a BMW-run F1 GTR in 1997, while a fourth place for Gulf again would prove the F1 GTR's swansong in 1998 as a new generation of LMP1 prototypes and purpose-built GT1 challengers came to the fore.

Across its three-year lifespan, the F1 GTR did enough to be considered as one of the all-time best British sports cars and, as Murray summarised: "Although we never planned for it, going racing actually turned out to be the perfect ending for the story of the McLaren F1." ●

McLaren's F1 GTR restoration project, immaculate in its Gulf Oils livery. MCLAREN

Family photo. Five generations of Le Mans-winning Audis lined up for show. From the R8 (back row) to the 2014 R18 e-tron quattro. AUDI SPORT

AUDI'S AGE OF DOMINATION

The formidable R8 and R10 turbodiesel set Audi on its way to celebrating 13 Le Mans victories, catapulting it from nowhere to be the second most successful manufacturer in the race's history. This is the story of both cars.

It was a rather understated debut, in all truth. All the headlines lay elsewhere. BMW had scored its one and so far only Le Mans victory using F1 tech from Williams and Mercedes' rocket ship CLRs took that designation a bit too seriously by literally reaching for the stars. Safe to say Le Mans 1999 was an eventful one.

But through it all, it would be the cars that finished a rather muted third and fourth that would go on to become the real story. There wasn't much hype about Audi's original R8Rs. They were rather humdrum-looking prototypes, two open-topped and two coupé. They qualified almost five seconds off the pace and simply kept things

clean to scoop a podium. Hardly the blazing kindling that would be the forerunner to the most dominant run Le Mans has ever witnessed.

But what the R8Rs did was convince Audi to take things further. They were the fuel on the bonfire and Ingolstadt lit the match with its second effort, the game-changing R8 of 2000.

Fast forward to the end of the R8's lifecycle in 2006 and it had racked up an unprecedented five wins at the 24 Hours and a total of 63 wins from the 79 races it took part in. It's one of, if not *the* greatest, returns for any sports car ever.

So how did Audi do it – from that understated 1999 debut to becoming king of La Sarthe just 12 months later?

Birth of the R8

While the R8 only came to prominence from 2000, the programme's roots stretch back to 1997 when multiple global brands such as Mercedes-Benz, McLaren, Porsche, Ferrari, BMW, Toyota and Nissan were gearing up for Le Mans projects.

Audi wanted in and announced its intention to join for 1999, so began work on a new concept alongside Italian manufacturer Dallara. That machine was the R8R and would become the test bed for Audi's new programme.

At the time the FIA and ACO was shifting the focus of Le Mans away from the GT1 class by removing the need for strict production runs for homologation. That instead allowed manufacturers to build one-off specials, signalling the rise of open-topped prototypes.

However, with coupé machines like the Toyota GT-One, Mercedes CLK-GTR and Porsche 911 GT1 still setting the pace, Audi was unsure of the best way forward for its new car, so it split its strategies. Five open-topped R8Rs were built and two chassis were sent to Audi's UK partner, Norfolk Racing Technology, to be turned into closed-top versions. The coupé R8C would also later be evolved into the base for the Bentley EXP Speed 8.

The R8R's first campaign in 1999 was a learning exercise. The aerodynamics constantly evolved with large changes to the front and rear bodywork and sidepods made almost race by race. The car lacked the outright pace of the Toyotas and BMWs, but did at least prove reliable. After Le Mans in 1999, the real work began.

Audi took the lessons from the R8R and put them into practice for the R8. The new design was truly ground-breaking, as Audi pursued reliability and accessibility over outright pace at first. The 3.6-litre petrol Audi engine was retained from the R8R.

The R8 was designed around a Dallara-built carbon monocoque, with an innovative design of rear chassis that enabled the team to service the car in extraordinary time. Spare rear assemblies would come complete with a rear subframe, six-speed gearbox, suspension and would be configured and weighted ready to be bolted on in the event of an accident.

Audi's partner team Joest Racing demonstrated the benefit, changing an entire rear assembly in just over three minutes, rather than a few hours.

Tom Kristensen conducted the early testing of the R8. He said: "We wanted reliability first and foremost. Audi had that German grit of always questioning things and wondering how the car would last in different situations. As a driver, when you know you have reliability underneath you, it's so important. You may not be the fastest on the straights or through corners but when you know you can take the car to the limit lap after lap and it wouldn't suffer or break it gives you a great advantage.

"I tested the interim R8, which was an R8R with the new rear-end bolted on and we

The R8 proved to be the most successful car in Le Mans history, paving the way for the R10's arrival (centre). The Team Goh car is on the left, with Champion Racing on the right. AUDI SPORT

Victory in 2002. Audis filled five of the top seven spots. AUDI SPORT

knew from the start it was special. It was quite a soft car that rode the bumps well and was comfortable. Usually if you ran a sports car too soft, it would become edgy and unstable, but the R8's chassis was so compliant and versatile.

By the end you could take it to Monza and strip the aero down and it would work, or go to the Nürburgring and pile the aero back on and it would work. It was a superb all-rounder."

Perfect timing

Audi's goal of winning Le Mans may have been made simpler by the withdrawal of many factory teams. Mercedes-Benz walked after its CLRs took flight and both Toyota and BMW were lured to Formula 1.

That left the way clear for Audi to shine, but even if the other brands had stayed, they would have faced one hell of a fight, such was the engineering detail of the R8. And where better to prove reliability out of the box but the car-breaking bumps of Sebring?

With no European Le Mans Series or world sports car championship to speak of, Audi did the majority of its development work in America. Allan McNish handled an R8 alongside Italian Rinaldo 'Dindo' Capello for that first season of the American Le Mans Series. The pair lifted the drivers' title.

"It may seem odd that a car built to win in Europe was honed in America, but the ALMS campaigns added a lot to the R8's development," said McNish. "The circuits in the US were very harsh and by running regularly on them we

Road America... with no suitable European championships, Audi honed the R10 in the USA, conquering the car-breaking bumps of Sebring. AUDI SPORT

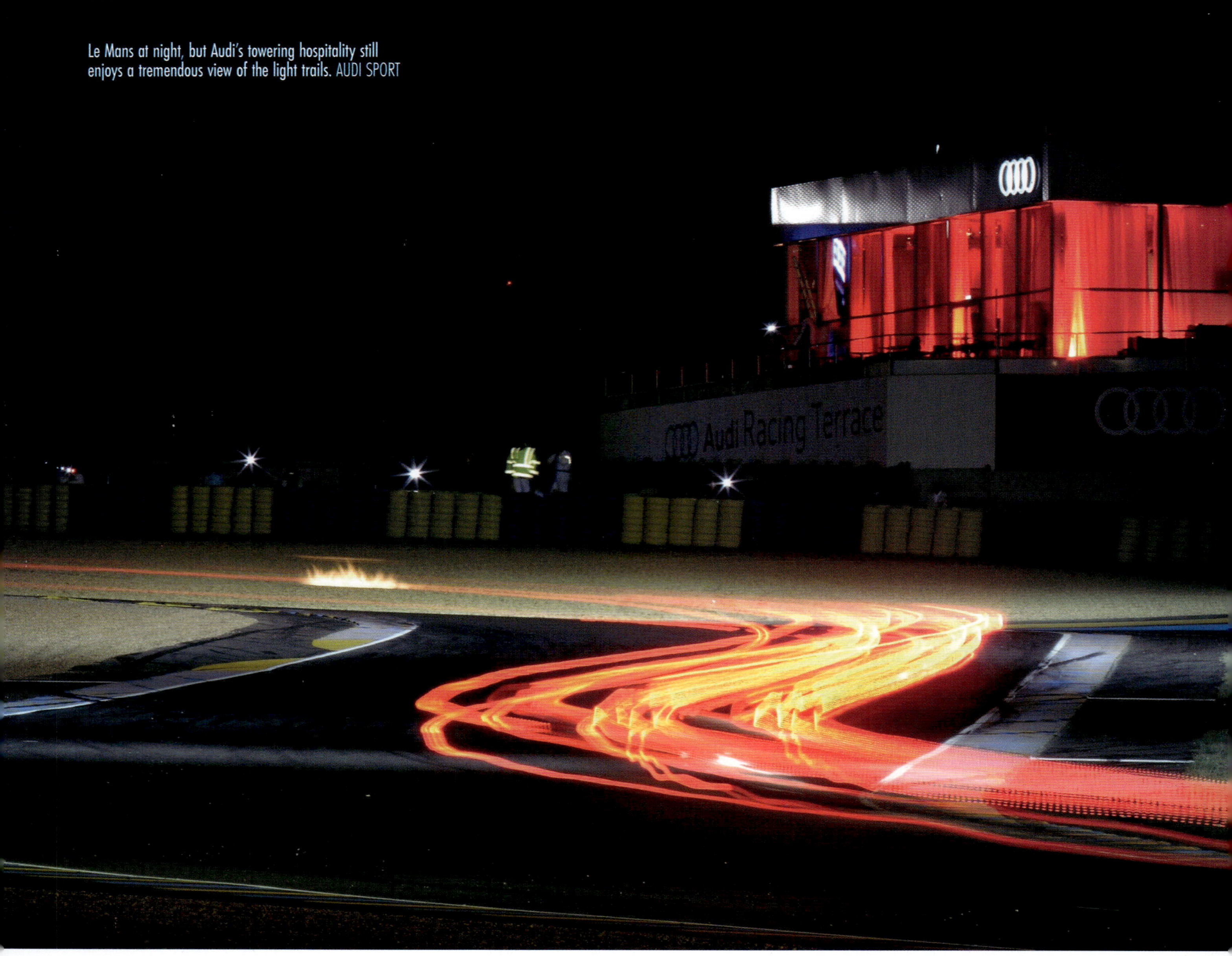

Le Mans at night, but Audi's towering hospitality still enjoys a tremendous view of the light trails. AUDI SPORT

built a very durable and adaptable car. When we got back to Europe we found we had a base in the R8 that was adaptable to dry, wet, hot, cold, bumpy, smooth – the car worked in every conceivable condition.

"At the start, it was a hard car to drive. At the 2000 Le Mans test it spat me off with a rear damper failure. While the results across its life make it look like plain sailing, it really wasn't. the engine had lots of power but wasn't the most compliant at the start and by Christ that power hit you when it came in. But the R8 suited my style. It was raw and you had to throw it around and tell it 'I'm the bloody boss, not you!'.

"We improved the aero a lot, mostly through adding ultimate downforce. I stopped driving the car after 2000 and went off to F1, but when I came back the R8's development curve had made it such a well-oiled car. The gear changes were better and Michelin had produced a great tyre. We'd introduced FSI [fuel injection] by then too, which removed a lot of the turbo lag and made drivability better and improved fuel consumption."

The R8 would go on to win Le Mans five times, every one with Kristensen at the wheel, and swept the board in the ALMS. And Audi's method of happily selling customer cars – similar to Porsche's business plan with the 956/962 – meant that even when its works team took a break, its customers kept up the business of winning where it mattered.

But the R8's day in the sun began to fade by the middle of the decade. The ACO banned the use of complete rear assembly swaps for 2003, demanding cars finish Le Mans with the gearbox they started with. Various other

Frank Biela, Emanuele Pirro and Marco Werner did the double at Le Mans with the R10 in 2006-07. AUDI SPORT

Three-time Le Mans winner Allan McNish. AUDI SPORT

step-change from the R8. And it just seemed like the natural solution.

Baretzky took it to the board, and went on to tell *Motor Sport*: "They must have thought I was crazy. Whenever I suggested it, they looked at me as though to say, 'You're an honourable man and have been successful, but isn't this a bit too much… a little too strange?'"

Turned out it wasn't. The VW Group board loved it. Diesel was en vogue at the time, being lauded for its mileage and efficiency and it was road relevant. There wasn't much not to love. Work began in 2004, but it was a mammoth task.

The rules allowed for a maximum capacity of 5.5-litres, so that's what Audi plumped for, running a road engine relentlessly on its test bench while it developed the race version of the V12, which was first fired up in May 2005.

The R10's body may have shared visual cues with the R8, but it was an all-new design. The monocoque build was brought in-house and the wheelbase was lengthened to accommodate the larger twin-turbo TDI engine. Audi's efforts were helped when the ACO raised the LMP1 minimum weight limit from 900 to 925kg for 2006, chiefly to allow air conditioning to be fitted to coupé cars.

Dr Wolfgang Ullrich. AUDI SPORT

ABOVE and BELOW: The revolutionary Audi TDI diesel engine, with glowing turbo. AUDI SPORT

rule tweaks were brought in to further reduce the R8's advantage, such as adding ballast and smaller engine restrictors. After its final win in 2005, the R8 was retired, only for a perhaps even greater beast to succeed it.

The 'monstrous' R10

Throughout history some of the greatest plans have been thought up in a bar, but at the time even this one sounded plain daft.

"My first instinct was to break out my little black book and find somewhere else to go!" recalls McNish of the moment he was first told that Audi was about to go diesel. "I never thought diesel could replace petrol at Le Mans. It added too much weight and wasn't as powerful, so I had huge doubts. But then they showed us some figures from the dyno and wind tunnel…"

In the early 2000s, Audi Sport head Dr Wolfgang Ullrich was discussing with the ACO how the rules could be opened up to embrace new technologies at Le Mans. And that got Audi engine boss Ulrich Baretzky thinking. During that night in the bar, Baretzky was joined by two important ACO members, Daniel Poissenot and Daniel Perdix. The concept of diesel came up and it stayed with Baretzky until the time Audi needed a

Tom Kristensen became the most successful Le Mans driver ever with Audi, winning five times with the R8 to bring his total to nine victories. AUDI SPORT

First and third on Le Mans debut in 2006, not a bad return for the new R10 TDI. AUDI SPORT

Kristensen said it transformed the way drivers found lap time: "We fitted the spool to control the weight under braking and on corner entry. The downside was that the spool meant a fully locked differential that led to mid-corner understeer quite often, so the driving style changed massively.

"Now it's all about momentum and flow and the transition of trail-braking and smooth acceleration. With the R10 it was about braking very late and aggressively and trying to get the car stopped and pointing in the right direction and then flooring it again. It wasn't about momentum, it was about stopping, steering and releasing the power in the most manageable way. In the early days we had issues with getting on the power and losing the chassis over bumps, so we had some very challenging steps and went through a fair bit of bodywork at first. The power was just unreal but as the car developed it became more drivable.

"The power band wasn't narrow, like on a road car, because you just had so much of it. We would wheelspin up the gears in a straight line if we weren't careful as we were sat on 1,200Nm of torque in a car that weighed 925kg. It was an experience to say the least."

The R10 broke boundaries. It won on its debut at the 2006 Sebring 12 Hours and at Le Mans both factory cars annexed the front row, two seconds clear of the competition. Audi took a 1-3 finish at La Sarthe, with the car of Frank Biela, Marco Werner and Emanuele Pirro winning and the Capello/McNish/Kristensen car losing time with fuel pump damage.

McNish reckons that first R10 win sparked the change in attitudes to alternative fuel in motorsport in general, not just at Le Mans. He said: "One week after the Sebring win, which was the first-ever international win for a diesel sportscar, Max Mosley [then FIA president] publicly stated that F1 should look to other areas and must be more aware of the environment. All of that was directly linked to what we did with the R10 TDI. I don't think we just changed sportscar racing, it started a trend and that victory at Sebring, and the one at Le Mans, was the game-changer.

"The Achilles Heel of the R10 was the fact that it was heavier than anything else," said Kristensen. "But it wasn't just because of the engine. You had to mobilise the extra torque so the driveshafts needed to be triple the usual size and the gearbox differential had to be much larger. Getting the weight distribution right was the biggest challenge."

McNish added: "Just like the R8, the R10 had loads of potential, but we had to refine it. It was very difficult to drive at first, mainly due to the monstrous power and torque. It marked the first time Michelin had developed a tyre for coping with that level of load. At the start we ran with no traction control because nobody had made one for a diesel prototype.

"The first time we tested in the wet, we were all trying to palm it off on each other because we thought it would be undrivable. But actually, the driving style made it very compliant in slippery conditions. You used the torque to pull you out of corners, then got on the power on the straights. It took us about a year to really learn how to drive it."

To counter the additional weight, Audi fitted a spool differential to aid handling.

Quite the photo finish in 2013. R18s would finish first, third and fifth, punctuated by the new Toyotas. AUDI SPORT

Peugeot proved a big-hitter against Audi. This is the factory team in 2011. PEUGEOT SPORT

"People became quite fascinated about how a car that was so fast just whispered as it went by. We had a lot of trouble with the GT cars not hearing us coming alongside and being so low that they couldn't see us. You had two schools of people – those who thought the R10 was soulless with no passion and noise and those who were taken in by the shock of its performance. I like to think we converted both as it was a racing showcase."

The R10 won Le Mans for three successive years and dominated Sebring until its retirement at the end of 2009, to be replaced with the remodelled R15 TDI, which was needed to counter the rising threat from another diesel-fuelled powerhouse.

Peugeot sparks the diesel wars

Audi wasn't the only one that saw the potential of racing with diesel power and Peugeot unveiled its 908 HDI FAP in 2005, with the intention of going head-to-head with Audi for glory two years later.

The drive behind the 908 programme came from the FAP part of the name, standing for particulate filter technology, which Peugeot was developing at the time. But the French manufacturer barely even had a racing team in place when the project got the green light, with many of its staff from the old 905 Group C era having moved on, including racing boss Jean Todt.

Regardless, Peugeot worked closely with renowned carbon composite chassis constructor Capricorn and together created the beautiful closed-cockpit 908. Together with its carbon monocoque, Peugeot developed its own 5.5-litre V12, with each engine bank cantered at 100-degrees to lower the centre of gravity.

With Audi pursuing the open-topped route, Peugeot saw more benefit in going coupé for its aero concept. The 908 proved impressively slippery on its Le Mans Series debut at Monza in 2007 – a circuit that rewards low downforce and high speed – claiming pole and a clear win. But not against Audi, which was still in America. The first head-to-head would come at the 24 Hours and Peugeot expected big things.

"The closed-cockpit was born for driver safety and aerodynamic efficiency," said engineer François Coudrain in an interview with *Car*. "The diesel engine was incredible in terms of torque – for the drivers it would hit them the minute they left the pits and deactivated the pitlane speed limiter. The aero regs then were quite open, so we could develop a very efficient car while trying to optimise the weight and centre of gravity."

Peugeot would top both testing and qualifying on its Le Mans debut, aided by a notable top-speed advantage along the three sections of the Mulsanne. The performance raised hopes of a French win on the marque's return. But it wouldn't come to fruition thanks to a combination of rear hub and oil pressure issues. The only works car left running finished second, 10 laps down on Audi.

Audi rains at Le Mans

The 2008 race should have gone Peugeot's way. The three works 908s were fantastically fast on the straights, lapping over five seconds

Peugeot's high came in 2009 when it took a one-two at Le Mans, with Alexander Wurz/Marc Gene/David Brabham coming out on top. PEUGEOT SPORT

up the road to the Audis. But in the race persistent rain removed that advantage and in an effort to boost downforce and grip Peugeot fitted modified bodywork that contributed to overheating. With the Peugeot engines turned down, Audi won again, somehow beating a brace of 908s to the flag in an epic duel.

But then came 2009 and Peugeot's moment of redemption. Even though new rules had been brought in to cut the power of the diesels, Peugeot claimed its third-straight Le Mans pole as Audi's new R15 faltered on its Le Mans debut, with its low-downforce bodywork backfiring. Audi drivers complained of understeer and excessive tyre wear, with some calling for a return to the high-downforce bodywork the car had run in Sebring. Over the race distance Peugeot would canter clear, with the 908 HDI FAP of Marc Gene/Alex Wurz/David Brabham leading a one-two.

Briton Antony Davidson joined the works team for the 2010 season and fell in love with the 908: "That was *my* car. That was my baby. It was made for me, just an absolute beast of a thing. Lower, wider, huge power and torque from the diesel. It made you feel like a hero. I felt like Steve McQueen every time I got in it. 1,250Nm of torque at 3,000rpm and 800bhp. It was so, so fast. Yet I could dominate it and just pull lap times from it whenever I wanted."

Yet Le Mans in 2010 didn't go to plan. Again the 908s were rampant with the three works cars and even the customer Oreca car filling the top four grid slots. But one lost time with

Peugeot locked out the front row against Audi in 2010, but there would be no repeat of the 2009 victory. PEUGEOT SPORT

Ex-F1 driver Anthony Davidson on duty with Peugeot, prior to his move to Toyota. PEUGEOT SPORT

The last hurrah for Peugeot's LMP1 team came in 2011. It was even testing a brand-new car when its 2012 programme was pulled. PEUGEOT SPORT

a failed alternator, another retired with broken suspension mounts after a series of kerb strikes, the Oreca car lost a driveshaft and then the race-leading #2 stopped with flames licking from its engine bay after a connecting rod failure. It was a miserable collapse as Audis filled the podium,

For 2011, Peugeot actually produced a brand-new car, still called the 908, but with sweeping updates, including an all-new 3.7-litre diesel powerplant. That car showed heaps of promise, running toe-to-toe with Audi's heavily reworked R18 TDI at Le Mans in 2011. All four cars would finish, but in formation from second-fifth as Audi's lead car once again just held on by a handful of seconds.

That battle should have continued into 2012, with the 908's diesel being supplemented by a new hybrid system under the new rules. The Peugeot Sport team was even out testing with the new cars at Sebring when the call came: the factory had pulled funding due to declining road car sales. Game over – and with it ended one of the great Le Mans rivalries. ●

It was the best of times, it was the worst of times: Audi and Peugeot monopolise the top places at the start in 2011. AUDI SPORT

It may not have been as radical to look at as some of its successors, but the R10 TDI laid the foundation for all of Audi's diesel dominance. AUDI SPORT

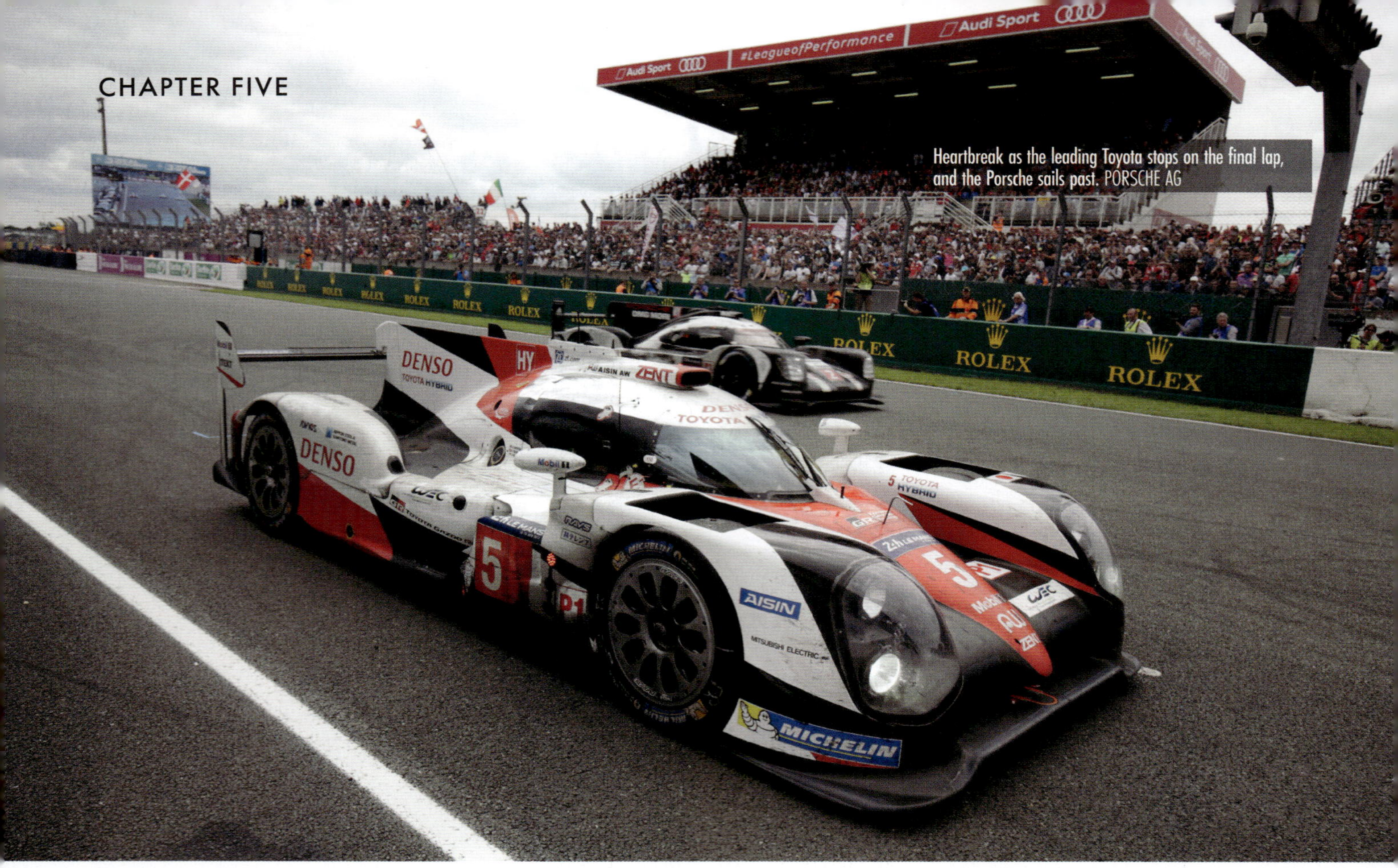

Heartbreak as the leading Toyota stops on the final lap, and the Porsche sails past. PORSCHE AG

THE GREATEST LOSS

Back in 2016, Toyota won the Le Mans 23 Hours 57 minutes. Having controlled the late stages of the race, the Japanese brand's TS050 Hybrid fell agonisingly short of an overall victory, in a dramatic twist that shocked the world

Three minutes equates to less than a lap of the Circuit de la Sarthe in a modern LMP1 car. Doesn't sound like much in the scope of a 24-hour race, but that's what proved the chasm that undid Toyota back in 2016.

The racing world held its collective breath when Toyota Gazoo Racing's number five TS050 Hybrid crawled its way out of the Ford chicane, just past the start-finish line to begin the final lap of the race, before then grinding to a halt right in front of the Toyota pit.

The effects became immediately clear as team boss Hughes de Chaunac crumbled to tears in the garage amidst a crowd of inconsolable mechanics. Engineers shouted into radio headsets as hands waved furiously at screens, but all to no avail. Anybody fan who says they didn't have a lump in their throat when driver Kazuki Nakajima had to be helped from the stranded car beset by grief is fibbing. This is a Le Mans memory so poignant, so painful, that it will stick with everybody witnessed it, regardless of which team they were backing.

In contrast, Porsche could hardly believe its luck. Its lead 919 Hybrid was languishing some

A disbelieving Toyota pitwall can only look on at the stranded car. TOYOTA GAZOO RACING

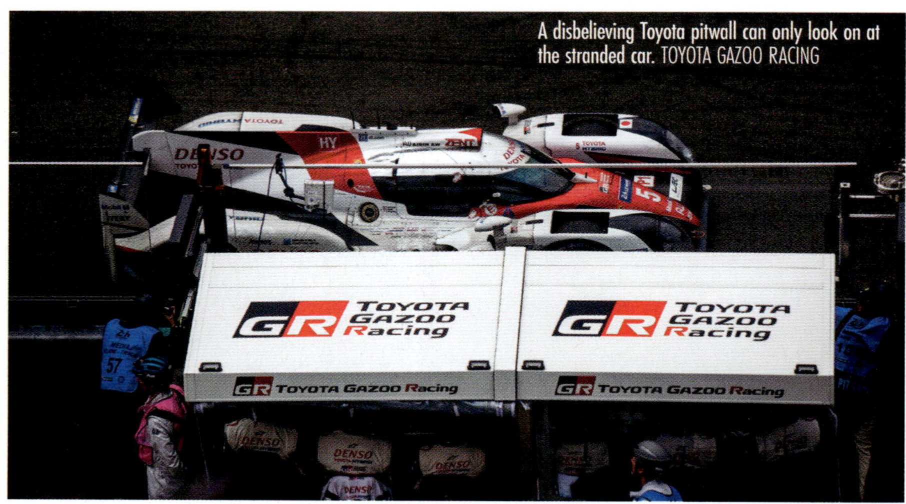

30 seconds back just a few moments ago, yet it had just been handed an historic 18th win, out of nowhere.

"Le Mans 2016 will stay with me forever, it was just incredibly cruel," said Nakajima, who was in control at the wheel, yet powerless to do anything. Nakajima and team-mates Sébastien Buemi and Anthony Davidson had until that point produced a near-perfect race.

Porsche's 919 Hybrid was faster over a lap, but Toyota played an effective game of fuel strategy to create a tense cat-and-mouse fight between its #5 car and the #2 Porsche of Neel Jani/Romain Dumas/Marc Lieb.

Having survived the night, catastrophe would strike Toyota the next afternoon. TOYOTA GAZOO RACING

Toyota president Akio Toyoda was also distraught, but countered the failure by saying: "We do not compete without knowing the feeling of loss. Having tasted the true bitterness of losing, we will return to the World Endurance Championship and the battle that is the Le Mans 24 Hours. For our quest is to build ever-better cars. For this, we will certainly come back to the roads of Le Mans."

And return it did. Porsche may have scored a record 19th Le Mans win during a topsy-turvy event in 2017, which featured a stripped-back LMP1 entry after the loss of Audi following the VW Group's 'Dieselgate' scandal, but when Porsche also pulled the plug a year later Toyota was left virtually uncontested in LMP1.

Still, as 2016 will attest, a Le Mans victory is still never a guarantee. The cars must still be built to survive the rigours of La Sarthe and Toyota proved more than up to the task, finally scoring its breakthrough Le Mans win in 2018, kick-starting the brand's current five-year winning streak.

Nakajima, finally, admitted there was an upside: "I think we gained more fans from losing that race than we ever would have gained if we'd won it! It turned out to be the start of a good story for Toyota." ●

Into that final hour, Nakajima emerged comfortably ahead and everything seemed to be going to plan. Japan was set to have its first Le Mans winner since the shock sprung by the Mazda 787B of 1991. And then fate intervened.

Nakajima got on the radio to the team reporting a loss of power as the Toyota started its penultimate lap then dramatically slowed down the Mulsanne Straight, barely managing to top 120mph at all on a section of track where drivers are usually pushing twice that.

"I couldn't believe what was going on," he said. "I had the engineers on the radio and we were trying to fix it. I still believed we could do something. I had to stop the car and restart."

Nakajima pulled over after the second chicane to power cycle the car – a traditional 'turn it off and on again' approach to clearing electrical bugs. The car refired and picked up some speed, but not for very long. Nakajima got round the rest of the lap before the car died entirely just metres onto the last lap of the race. Jani's Porsche 919 Hybrid sped by at full tilt, and the Porsche team exploded while Toyota crumbled.

"Absolute kicker"

"I've lost Le Mans in a lot of ways, but 2016 was the absolute kicker," said Davidson. "I feel I did everything in my power to win that race but it wasn't meant to be. We executed a perfect race to that point, so I still consider us the moral winners of Le Mans that year. We don't need the trophy to tell us we won it. But you couldn't have written that ending, nobody would have believed it if it had been a movie. To actually live it was pretty hard to take."

Nakajima continued: "At the end I was actually quite calm – no more shouting, no more panicking, but there was a lot of emotion."

The team eventually managed to get the car running to at least complete a final lap. However, Le Mans rules at the time demanded a car's final lap must be completed in a maximum of six minutes. Nakajima could only crawl round in just short of 12, so the car wasn't even classified. The ACO has since altered this rule.

Toyota sent the car back to base for a full investigation, eventually tracing the failure back to a faulty connector between the intercooler and the turbocharger, which caused a gradual decline in power and then eventually a total loss of drive. What amounted to a few pence-worth of component caused a multi-million-pound car to fail at the worst possible moment.

Disbelief in the joy. Porsche drivers Romain Dumas and Marc Lieb can't believe their luck. PORSCHE AG

A distraught Nakajima is helped from his stricken Toyota. GETTY IMAGES

THE FUTURE IS
HERE

It's only taken a couple of decades to work out something that in theory is surprisingly simplistic. Come up with a single set of rules so that brands can build a sports-racing car to be used in both the FIA World Endurance Championship and IMSA in America. How hard could it be? Turns out, very…

To skip past a dollop of technical jargon, marketing spiel and the odd swirl of vested interest, the convergence endurance racing fans have been crying out for has finally arrived in the form of the Le Mans Hypercar. Well, that

and Le Mans Daytona Hypercar (or Hybrid, to IMSA fans who don't like the term, Hypercar), either way it's otherwise known as LMDh.

Le Mans Hypercar (LMH) is a product of the FIA and ACO to create a new premier category to replace the now-mothballed LMP1 class. LMDh then came to life as a sort of halfway house to allow manufacturers that are perhaps on a more restricted budget or just more interested in IMSA and the North American market to also travel across to Europe for a shot at the holy grail of racing marketing that is a Le Mans 24 Hours victory.

Together, LMH and LMDh boil down to two different ways of building a car to run under a single rule set. The WEC and Le Mans will quite happily allow LMDh cars to run alongside Hypercars and vice-versa for IMSA, giving European teams the prospect of competing at prestige Stateside events like the Daytona 24 Hours, Sebring 12 Hours and Petit Le Mans. The rules were cleared from the start of this season, but expect the crossover to really start from 2024 as this year will be used to gauge how new balance of performance rules will be used to make sure

The new unified era of sportscar racing roars away at Sebring, with Toyota, Ferrari, Porsche, Cadillac, Peugeot and more in the fray. GETTY IMAGES

Since the arrival of the new Hypercar regulations, the buzz is well and truly back at Le Mans. Manufacturers are flooding back and grids are filling up. But what is a Hypercar, who's involved and what does the future hold? We endeavour to find out.

the different types of cars can compete on an equal footing.

While some LMDh cars have already featured at Daytona back in January, this new unified era of top-flight sportscar racing got rolling proper with the WEC season opener at Sebring in March where Hypercars and LMDh ran as one for the first time.

What is a Le Mans Hypercar?

Easy...ish. Put simply, the Le Mans Hypercar rules allow manufacturers the freedom to design and build their own chassis, engine and optional hybrid systems under a basic set of parameters – such as minimum weight, maximum power and aerodynamic performance.

This is unquestionably the more expensive option, but it also has the most room for innovation. Chassis rules are far more open, so manufacturers can use either an existing racing chassis or the base of a road-going hypercar (Aston Martin Valkyrie, Mercedes-AMG One, etc) and into that they can plonk any engine they like (so long as it's not a diesel, as we're over that now). The only stipulation is that the unit can't produce more than 670bhp in race trim. Hybrid systems

can be freely developed, and used to supplement a maximum boost of 268bhp to either the rear axle or the front (to create temporary four-wheel drive) when the car is travelling northwards of 75mph.

Bodywork is a big part of the appeal, as manufacturers are encouraged to style their prototypes using cues from their road car designs in a move away from the alien-like LMP1 spaceships.

What is an LMDh?

Many of the basics mentioned above still apply here, but the process is more simplistic. Instead of

New era, same result. Toyota took a masterful one-two at Sebring to lay down the gauntlet to its new challengers. TOYOTA GAZOO RACING

spending big bucks creating bespoke composite chassis, manufacturers must use an off-the-shelf chassis from one of four nominated suppliers as a base – Dallara, Multimatic, Ligier or Oreca.

Within the spec chassis, manufacturers must use an engine from a recognised supplier, so there are no ground-breaking innovations here, simply plug and play, as is the demanded Xtrac gearbox. Added to the engine is a spec hybrid system developed by Bosch and Williams Advanced Engineering, which will send a constant stream of hybrid power through the rear axle alone when the car is running. To wrap it all up, manufacturers are again free to clothe the prototype how they wish, including brand-specific styling. This method has proven incredibly popular at bringing brands back to the grid, with the likes of Porsche and BMW joining IMSA regulars Acura and Cadillac for this year and many more big names busy developing their own contenders.

What's happened so far?

The Le Mans Hypercar rules came into effect for 2021 in Europe, but have been a bit of a slow-burner due to the ongoing negotiations between WEC and IMSA about which cars could do what and where, but now the flame has firmly been lit.

The first two years were all about Toyota, which quickly established a monopoly on both the world championship and Le Mans, challenged only by the privateer Glickenhaus team and an effort from

Alpine, which was allowed to run an updated LMP1 chassis while it evaluated committing to its own Hypercar programme. With the Alpine hamstrung by some hybrid and fuel restrictions, Toyota never really had much to overcome and cantered to two back-to-back one-two finishes at Le Mans in 2021 and 2022.

But this year is a different story. Ferrari is back for 2023 after a 50-year hiatus from the

top class of Le Mans. Peugeot has returned with a radical wingless new design, plus there's a new privateer effort from Vanwall (read ByKolles, a long-term entrant in LMP1), plus LMDh entries from both Cadillac and Porsche. With an entry list twice as big for this year, and set to expand again for 2024, continued success will be hard-earned for Toyota. Just the way the team likes it…

Toyota has had a monopoly on Le Mans in recent years, being challenged last year by just the privateer Glickenhaus and ageing Alpine LMP1. That's soon set to change. TOYOTA GAZOO RACING

THE CLASS OF 2023

With so many new and familiar faces, it can be tough to keep track of who's running what and when. Here we take a look at the contenders for 2023 and beyond.

TOYOTA
Class: Hypercar
Car: GR010 Hybrid
Drivers: #7 Mike Conway/Kamui Kobayashi/José María López; #8 Sébastien Buemi/Brendon Hartley/Ryo Hirakawa

Unquestionably the benchmark for this season, not just because it's essentially had a two-year head-start on everybody else, but because the Toyota Gazoo Racing squad has evolved into the slickest endurance racing outfit in the world. You only need look at the season opener in Sebring to see that.

As the first Hypercar, the GR010 has undergone a steady series of updates, such as swapping the original 14in wheels all-round to 12.5in fronts and 14in rears to make better use of the four-wheel-drive hybrid system last year, and this year's version goes even further. The car's gone on a diet all-round to finally get down to the 1,040kg minimum weight. The 3.5-litre turbocharged engine has been reworked to improve efficiency and power delivery, as has the hybrid system. The bodywork has sprouted new downforce-inducing diveplanes at the front and smaller rear wing endplates, plus there are additional cooling vents for the brakes and a revised headlight layout to aid racing at night.

It all sparks of evolution rather than revolution, because that's all Toyota really needs as its key strength lies in the core team in and around the cars. It has six of the most proven and reliable sportscar drivers on the planet, plus a sound management team and incredibly efficient technical crews.

Take Sebring as an example. Yes, Ferrari was faster in qualifying, but when the race got going the Toyotas produced a metronomic performance that blew the Italians into the weeds. Not a single missed step across eight hours of racing, ending up with another one-two and a two-lap gap to the rest shows just how much of a mountain everybody else needs to climb to tackle Toyota.

Team technical director Pascal Vasselon summed up Toyota's approach, saying: "The updates to the car are the normal next step for us, but it is exciting to compete against new entrants in Hypercar this year. But our approach doesn't change. The job remains the same: we aim to win, so we must get the maximum from our package, without mistakes."

FERRARI
Class: Hypercar
Car: 499P
Drivers: #50 Antonio Fuoco/Miguel Molina/Nicklas Nielsen; #51 Alessandro Pier Guidi/James Calado/Antonio Giovinazzi

Putting the 'hype' into Hypercar. There have been few sports cars more eagerly anticipated then this one and so far it's shown all the right signs. Not only does Ferrari's first entry to the top class at Le Mans for 50 years look stunning, it's also got decent pace.

Less prancing horse, more galloping one. Ferrari's new 499P looks stunning, and fast so far FERRARI

Toyota's updates may be subtle, but the GR010 Hybrid is still the class of the field, and by some way TOYOTA GAZOO RACING

The Scuderia's last top-flight factory effort at La Sarthe was the 312PB of 1973, crewed by Carlos Pace/Arturo Merzario, which qualified on pole and went on to finished second. The 499P didn't quite manage to match that exactly, but had to make do with a pole and a third place, which isn't half bad against a team as well-drilled as Toyota.

Running Ferrari's bespoke chassis with a three-litre twin-turbo engine and hybrid front axle to create temporary four-wheel drive, the 499P should have the firepower to take on Toyota in a straight fight, proven when Fuoco scorched to pole by over two tenths in Florida. The race may have gone askew, with a botched early pit stop losing Fuoco the lead and then a couple of penalties for bread-and-butter infractions (overtaking before the start line under the safety car and a pit infringement) left the best car third, a long way off the runaway Toyotas.

But, as driver James Calado says, expectations must be managed. Let's not forget it took Toyota years to get into the winning form it enjoys now.

"This season is shaping up to be an incredible one, perhaps the toughest in history," said Calado. "We know we're facing a huge challenge. This is a brand new programme, with a new car and we likely won't know where we truly stand until somewhere around the third race."

It's also a steep learning curve, as the AF Corse team that has run the Ferrari factory efforts in the GT classes steps up to the top class with just a single season of LMP2 prototype racing under its belt.

"There's some adapting to do," added Calado, a three-time WEC champion in the GT ranks. "For the team, the engineers I know are learning the Hypercar quickly and there's already been a big step up in Ferrari. We've got a lot more working flat-out day and night on this project. We're at a level that's much like F1. We've got the right guys behind us to get what we want, which is to win races and championships with Ferrari on the biggest stage in sportscar racing."

Cadillac
Class: LMDh
Car: V-LMDh
Drivers: #2 Earl Bamber/Alex Lynn/ Richard Westbrook; #3 Sébastien Bourdais/Renger van der Zande/TBA; #311 (Action Express Racing) Luis Felipe Derani/Alexander Sims/Jack Aitken

It's been over 20 years since Cadillac last went head-to-head with the European brands at Le Mans, but this year there's set to be three of its new V-LMDh contenders on the grid at La Sarthe, split between two for the factory team and one for Action Express Racing. And, if the car goes anywhere near as well in Europe as it has done so far in America, then the General Motors brand could be a genuine threat.

Cadillac's Le Mans history isn't stellar, given its best-ever finish is ninth place on its final attempt back in 2002. But its new V-LMDh is an entirely different proposition. Cadillac's main programme is IMSA, where it will field two cars, with a single-car entry in the full WEC season, ahead of that triple-threat entry at Le Mans.

Unlike many of its rivals, Cadillac has eschewed the typical turbo power for something more familiar, a hulking 5.5-litre V8 that sits within its Dallara-built chassis. WEC driver Alex Lynn reckons the usually large engine capacity has its benefits: "It produces a lot of power and a lot of torque. The biggest advantage is the drivability. The power delivery is very smooth, very linear and the traction is very good. We don't have any turbo spool or lag so we have power as and when we need it. The drawback comes when you want to lift and coast as there's a lot of engine braking and torque to wind down. These new cars have a lot less downforce than the old LMP1 cars did, but the same sort of power, so they can be quite wild to drive."

Having finished third, fourth and fifth at Daytona on its debut, the V-LMDh also impressed during the WEC opener at Sebring. While it couldn't match the pace of the Toyotas, in race trim the single car was a thorn in Ferrari's side throughout and nearly stole the final podium spot, beating back Porsche's new 963.

Peugeot
Class: Hypercar
Car: 9X8
Drivers: #93 Paul di Resta/Mikkel Jensen/ Jean Éric Vergne; #94 Loïc Duval/Gustavo Menezes/Nico Müller

Is it too early to use the word 'crisis'? Well, yes and no when it comes to Peugeot's already issue-plagued start to life in Hypercar. The French brand's 9X8 is a remarkable-looking thing. Wonderfully styled and the car was the talk of the sport when it was revealed with a total lack of rear wing. It's an interesting approach which Peugeot's aero bods insist gives the car an impressive blend of pure speed and aerodynamic stability, with the 9X8 designed to generate most of its downforce from the car's underbody, ground-effects style.

However, what looked good on paper hasn't translated to the track ... yet. The car made its competitive debut last year at Monza, the WEC event directly after Le Mans, aiming to use the final three races of the season to test and develop the new car. Its debut in Italy was plagued by electrical gremlins. And it didn't get much better as Peugeot failed to get either of its cars to the finish in the subsequent events without some form of reliability issue. Fourth places in both Fuji and Bahrain (seven and six laps down on the winning Toyota, respectively) were its best return.

Peugeot opted to spend the entirety of its winter testing in Europe, deciding against sending a 9X8 to the Sebring Prologue test. In doing so, Peugeot was essentially writing off Sebring, and for good reason. With its car so obviously tailored for the fast sweeps of Le Mans, the violent bumps of Sebring's former airfield track ruined any ground-effect the 9X8 would have, rendering the car largely uncompetitive. Yet it was still embarrassing for the team to lose one car on the formation lap with a gearbox fault, and have electrical issues strike the remaining one. While the rest of the Hypercar field romped to the finish, Peugeot was nowhere.

But let's not write Peugeot off yet. Don't forget when it started the 908 programme it

Cadillac's new LMDh could well be one to watch. Three will run at Le Mans, and it fared well at Sebring (below). GENERAL MOTORS

Perhaps it's just too radical? We've yet to see the best of Peugeot's 9X8, but it has huge potential. PEUGEOT SPORT

barely had a technical team in place, yet turned that into a Le Mans winner, so there's hope.

Porsche
Class: LMDh
Car: 963
Drivers: #5 Dane Cameron/Michael Christensen/Frédéric Makowiecki; #6 Kevin Estre/André Lotterer/Laurens Vanthoor; #38 (Hertz Team Jota) António Félix da Costa/Will Stevens/Yifei Ye; #75 Felipe Nasr/TBA/TBA

When it comes to expectations, those surrounding this car are sky high. Ferrari can be forgiven should it suffer a slow start after five decades away, but Porsche is a serial winner and any car with the nomenclature to follow the legendary 962 must have winning sewn into its carbon weave.

Porsche didn't muck about with the car's development. The 963 was technically ready to race last year if Porsche had wanted, but instead the Stuttgart brand opted to spend a full year pounding around doing endurance testing and has already started selling customer versions too (such as the Jota car that will appear at later WEC rounds and at Le Mans).

Somewhat surprisingly, Porsche opted to go down the LMDh route, but for a few clear reasons. Firstly cost, as it had been there and done it with $100m+ budgets during the LMP1 days, and secondly to major on the North American car market. Having a car that could run easily on both sides of the Atlantic was a must. Plus the ease of the LMDh build helps it create and sell customer cars, much in the same way it did with the 956 and 962s that went on to dominate Group C, and not always with the factory team.

Using the Multimatic chassis and a 4.5-litre twin-turbo V8, the 963 looked quick on its Daytona debut, but a combination of battery and gearbox issues put both out. The twin 963s made it to the finish at Sebring, but in fifth and sixth, and then could well have won the following Sebring 12 Hours had they not been taken out in a multi-car clash.

The WEC car did struggle to nurse its tyres on the Sebring bumps, with the rears dropping off during longer stints, making the 963s a handful. Still, with Sebring being an outlier in the calendar due to its rough and rugged nature, there's plenty of promise for the 963 heading into the European season. And, if nothing else, Porsche can fall back on having four of them on the grid at La Sarthe.

"It's just fantastic to see what's happening this year with all the new cars coming in and we know it will be a really tight season between all of us… it's a great time to be involved," said driver Frédéric Makowiecki. "Right now, we're in learning mode, much like everybody else."

What about the rest?

The remainder of the 16-car Hypercar entry for this year's Le Mans 24 Hours will be completed by cars from both the privateer Glickenhaus and Vanwall teams. These are both non-hybrid Hypercar entries that, quite frankly, don't look like making too much of an impact now that the big guns have arrived.

Glickenhaus' pretty 007s were a highlight of last year's WEC, taking the fight to the Toyotas and sneaking a podium finish at Le Mans. Glickenhaus should probably have won at Monza but for a turbo failure. But they've fallen on harder times since. The Pipo Moteurs-engined cars missed the final two races of the WEC last season on budgetary counts and have simply done nothing all winter. One car was taken to Sebring for the WEC opener but

Be honest, we're all rooting for it. Glickenhaus was a star last season, but has struggled this year. GETTY IMAGES

lagged behind the newer machinery, eventually stopping after a series of electrical issues. Two cars should make the trip to Le Mans, with so far only Romain Dumas and Franck Mailleux listed as drivers in what could well be the final hurrah for everybody's favourite 2022 underdog.

And then there's Vanwall (ByKolles). Colin Kolles' team has been working on this car since 2018, but few expected it to be relabelled Vanwall after the long-defunct British F1 team. And even fewer expected 1997 F1 World Champion Jacques Villeneuve to wind up in it! Sharing with Tom Dillmann and Esteban Guerrieri, the Canadian hasn't raced at Le Mans since his days with Peugeot in 2008. We didn't get to see too much of the Vanwall Vandervell 680 due to a cocktail of clashes and suspension troubles at Sebring, with Villeneuve saying: "it doesn't handle the bumps at all well… it constantly surprises you." Given ByKolles' abysmal record at Le Mans – it didn't finish the race at all in its nine attempts between 2010-2020 – don't expect miracles. ●

Talk about expectation. Porsche's 963 simply has to succeed, and you wouldn't bet against it. PORSCHE AG

WHAT DOES THE FUTURE HOLD?

Simply put: a lot. Those listed previous are just the field for this season. By 2025, we should be able to add BMW, Lamborghini, Alpine, Acura (Honda) and perhaps even classic Italian brand Isotta Fraschini to the grid.

BMW has already confirmed it will be at Le Mans next year with its M Hybrid V8, which is currently being developed as it races in IMSA, while Lamborghini is well down the road with developing its LMDh entry, working closely with Ligier on the design and has signed ex-F1 men Romain Grosjean and Daniil Kvyat as a statement. Acura is already running well as its new ARX-05 celebrated a one-two finish at Daytona, ahead of the Cadillacs. The issue is the branding of Honda's North American arm – would the cars run as Acuras at Le Mans, or be rebadged Hondas, and then who's paying for it? Regardless, teams like Meyer Shank and Wayne Taylor Racing have made it clear they'd like a crack at Le Mans, but without a full-season WEC entry on the horizon it becomes difficult.

Alpine has partnered with Oreca to build its own LMDh, having finally ditched the old ex-Rebellion LMP1 design it was running as a toe-in-the-water exercise during the last two WEC seasons. Its own engine is already running on the test bench.

Then there's the hugely left-field news that reborn Isotta Fraschini – a pre-war automaker with victory in the second-ever Targa Florio in 1908 to its name – is working on a full-blown Hypercar project and targeting races later this year. With a car built by ex-Ferrari factory partner Michelotto, the Vector Sport team applied for a WEC entry this year but couldn't secure one, so it is instead aiming to test and slip into a few one-off races before the year is out.

Add all that up and we could well be enjoying even more manufacturers vying for supremacy at Le Mans than even Group C managed in its heyday. But a word of warning – manufacturers are notoriously fickle when it comes to racing, so while it could also create a wonderful bubble for sports car fans, it's one that could also go pop at any time. Still, the promised proliferation of customer cars from brands like Porsche acts as a stabiliser should the factory teams walk. A lot of eyes will be on how the balance of performance is managed this year, too.

And then there's LMP2. With the LMDh cars already running on the next-generation LMP2 chassis, will the rise in customer cars essentially spell the end for what has regularly been Le Mans' most entertaining category? We certainly hope not.

Revolution is also well underway in the GT ranks, with the costly GTE (Grand Touring Endurance) cars being phased out in favour of adopting the global GT3 category instead. GTE Pro has gone for this year, leaving just GTE Am to run using a mixture of professional and amateur drivers while the switch in format is made ahead of next year.

This should have happened ages ago, such is the popularity of GT3 and the strength of both the customer and factory racing scene. Expect brands to be queueing up and most likely a return of the full professional class in the coming years, where factories will wheel out their finest GT drivers in works-backed cars. It should be spectacular.

The glory days of endurance racing aren't back just yet, but they're certainly on their way. Here's to the next 100 years of the Le Mans 24 Hours.